A Field of Tents
and
Waving Colours

Neville Cardus (1888–1975) was born in Rusholme, Manchester and began writing about cricket for the *Manchester Guardian* in 1919 when he was sent to cover a match at Old Trafford. He was also for many years the paper's chief music critic. His many books included *Days in the Sun*, *Good Days* and *Australian Summer*. He was knighted in 1966. In the eulogy at his memorial service the cricket historian Alan Gibson said that 'just as Macaulay changed the course of the writing of history, Cardus changed the course of the writing of cricket. He showed what could be done. He dignified and illuminated the craft.'

Gideon Haigh has been praised as 'our greatest living cricket writer'. His books include *Mystery Spinner*, his prizewinning biography of Jack Iverson, *The Big Ship*, on the life of the Australian Test captain Warwick Armstrong, and *Stroke of Genius*, about Victor Trumper. He lives in Melbourne, Australia.

A Field of Tents
and
Waving Colours

NEVILLE CARDUS
writing on Cricket

With an introduction by
Gideon Haigh

Edited by Graham Coster

SAFE HAVEN

*The publisher gratefully acknowledges the
assistance of Fiona Hertford-Hughes, copyright
holder of the Estate of Neville Cardus, in putting this
selection of his work together.*

First published 2019 by
Safe Haven Books Ltd
12 Chinnocks Wharf
42 Narrow Street
London E14 8DJ
www.safehavenbooks.co.uk

This paperback edition published 2020

A catalogue record for this book
is available from the British Library.

ISBN 978 1 916045 36 1

1 3 5 7 9 10 8 6 4 2

2020 2022 2024 2023 2021

Typeset in Filosofia by M Rules

Printed and bound in Great Britain by Clays Ltd, Elcograf S. p. A.

MIX
Paper from
responsible sources
FSC® C018072

Contents

Introduction

BY GIDEON HAIGH

For a long time, Sir Neville Cardus was regarded as cricket's greatest writer; then he wasn't. The two perspectives may be related. What one generation exalts, the next is almost bound to despise. But there is something odd about his fall from grace, because it often feels more concerned with whether it is 'OK' to like Cardus, and to arise from assumptions about Cardus rather than involving the effort of actually reading him.

To be fair, Cardus's canonical status was never universally agreed. 'Ah don't like thy writing, Mester Cardus,' Yorkshire's Arthur Mitchell purportedly reproached him. 'It's too fancy.' But he is especially ill-suited to these aggressively neophilial and levelling times. *Sir* Neville Cardus: why, the very name is anachronistic. He must have been a posh boy, mustn't he? Didn't he throw in allusions to classical music? Didn't he use fancy metaphors? Ignoring that classical music was in Cardus's time perfectly popular culture, not least in the Manchester of his boyhood. Ignoring that in reaching outside the sporting vernacular for a fresh perspective on participants and feats, Cardus was arguably more in tune with the sportswriting of today than his own.

Ah, but he was a snob, wasn't he? Now, there *is* something to this. Cardus was dedicated to the memory of the cricket and the cricketers of his pre-World War I youth, with a partiality to the pedigree amateur batsmen who defined it – or indeed, it should be said, who he helped define it, for it was Cardus who pressed into common coinage the notion of an Edwardian 'Golden Age of Cricket'. Likewise could he be nostalgically deprecating of what came after, a lamentation of 'the nation's lost peace and plenty'. He could be glib, facile. He was assuredly no historian – you would no sooner rely on factual actuality in a piece of Cardus's than in a Trump tweet.

But show me a sports writer not occasionally star-struck, not periodically jaded, who does not have favourites and harbour prejudices. At least Cardus's were sincere rather than sycophantic. When he derided Bloggs of Blankshire, furthermore, he was making a point every cricket watcher can understand – that there are players who hold, for all sorts of reasons, greater personal and aesthetic appeal than others. The scoreboard, he maintained, 'will not get anywhere near the secret of Woolley. It can only tell us about Bloggs.' Those greats, too, have better days than others: 'Only mediocrity is always at its best.'

Nowadays it is a term of approbation to refer to a sports writer as possessing the 'enthusiasm of the fan'. Cardus was here a pioneer. Few cricket writers have so often mentioned the perspective of an everyday spectator, for a simple reason: being not an ex-player, he was well acquainted with the cheap seats by the time he gravitated to journalism in his early thirties. So when he described the post-1947 Denis Compton, for example, he saw it from the terraces: 'In a world tired, disillusioned and bare, heavy with age and deprivation, this happy cricketer spread his favours everywhere, and thousands of us, young and old, ran his runs with him. Here at any rate was something unrationed. There were no coupons in an innings by Compton.'

Oh yes, one last thing: the parrot cry that Cardus 'made things up'. Some of his stories were too good to be true because they weren't. But literary licence, as Cardus's first biographer Christopher Brookes observed, is nothing so new: 'After all, Shakespeare missed Agincourt.' It's also worth considering the factual economy of Cardus's era, unassisted by the real-time stat and the media soundbite, based on the unaided eye versus the unyielding distance. Writing fifty years ago, Cardus had this to say about his starting out as a reporter of county cricket:

> Silence reigned supreme. There was no specialist statistician to inform us that so-and-so had bowled so many overs, or that so-and-so had completed his 50 in two and a half hours. We had to make our *own*

statistical recordings. Jimmy Catton, of the now defunct *Manchester Evening Chronicle*, himself wrote down a ball-by-ball analysis of each bowler, also detailing the value and direction of every stroke. So did all the other cricket reporters.

It was Cardus, in fact, who became the first correspondent to liberate cricket journalism from the menial transcription of action, who discerned in the game the scope for a literary imagination. Cardus is not, then, to be understood merely by his own writing, but from cricket in newspapers before and after him. Never before had press box journalism been worth reading for its own sake: as John Arlott put it, Cardus 'forced cricket into a position where the literate had to notice it, and, in doing so, compelled an improvement in the general standard of writing about the game'. He provided word pictures where there were as yet no serious photographs. He offered reflections on cricket's place in public affection where there was so far scant thought. And if this involved the occasional tactful fiction, then so did his life.

His real name was John Frederick Newsham. He was born illegitimate in 1888. He never knew his father, a smith, who left Manchester for America days after marrying his mother; he knew his mother, a prostitute, perhaps too well to write about her. He was haphazardly raised in a crowded semi by an extended family of launderers, minimally educated in a board school to the age of ten. It's a modern affectation of the successful to embroider their early CVs with mundane jobs because they pulled some call centre shifts and worked a night or two as a dish pig. Long before he started journalism as a penny-a-liner for Manchester's left-wing *Daily Citizen*, Fred Newsham was a jack-of-all-trades: he delivered washing from the family laundry, worked as a pavement artist, drove a joiners' handcart, boiled type in a printer's works, sold flowers on the street, confectionery in a theatre and funeral insurance door-to door.

How did such a leisured and picturesque style emerge from such a hardscrabble existence? The question may answer itself – the writing constituted an act of self-creation. Fred Newsham belongs in the tradition of autodidacticism, culturally conservative but insatiably curious, described by Jonathan Rose in his *The Intellectual Life of the British Working Classes*. Manchester had a huge university, great law courts. It was a musical city – the home of Sir Thomas Beecham, the headquarters of the Hallé and numerous smaller orchestras, of pantomimes that cannibalised opera, of pubs that nourished music hall. Its local authority had acquired an extensive gallery with a superb fine arts collection, the Manchester City Art Gallery, and been the first in Britain to endow public lending and reference libraries.

The Manchester Free Library's opening was attended by Charles Dickens. So was Fred Newsham's intellectual awakening. He 'went crazy' on discovering the novelist in Harmsworth shilling editions:

> It was scarcely a case of reading at all; it was almost an experience of a world more alive and dimensional than this world, heightened and set free in every impulse of nature; not subtle and abnormal impulses but such as even a more or less illiterate youth could at once share.

Dickens was then out of highbrow literary fashion — plots too sentimental, characters too caricatured. Youthful Newsham dared think otherwise: 'He [Dickens] simply let me see them more than life-size. David Copperfield so often behaved and thought as I behaved and thought that I frequently lost my own sense of identity in him.'

Fred Newsham allocated his new identity a new name. The Cardus scholar Christopher O'Brien reports that 'Neville Cardus' appeared for the first time in print in a journal called *Musical Opinion*: a December 1916 critique of the composer Granville Bantock appears under the byline 'J. F. Neville Cardus'. Cardus was his mother's surname; Neville was inspired, O'Brien conjectures, by the all-rounder John Neville Crawford, whose virtues the writer often later extolled. Arlott observed that Cardus understood the impression left by 'Neville' as distinct from 'Fred' — in the same way, perhaps, as 'Cyril James' understood himself better off as 'C. L. R'.

In that same month, Cardus applied successfully to C.

P. Scott for a job at the *Manchester Guardian*. He started in the reporters' room in March 1917, a spare pair of hands. Though Cardus loved cricket – in his mid-twenties, he had spent four summers as an assistant coach at Shrewsbury – there was none for him to report. It was after a 'breakdown' he suffered two years into his career that Scott's sympathetic lieutenant W. P. Crozier decided Cardus 'might recuperate myself by sitting in the air one or two days at Old Trafford' for the first county match since 1914.

'It was indeed easy to feel the sentimental aspect of the occasion,' the apprentice cricket writer began. 'One came into the enclosure from the dusty town, and there were for many an old cricket lover strong tugs on the heart as they saw again the soft green splashed with the spring sun and the red pavilion and the county flag streaming in the wind.' The sense of occasion; the sensitivity to the palette; the kinship with the crowd; the sense of what has gone before: these features of Cardus's writing were present from the very first. Also the attachment to the local, for he would remain a man of the north:

> In most matches the critic endeavours to be impartial; he sits aloft in the press-box, like an impersonal god, seeing all things moving, towards their predestined end. The Lancashire and Yorkshire match is an exception; I step down from the pedestal of impartiality . . . I have found that a partnership can often be broken by leaving the

press box and retiring for a moment (usefully) behind the scene. I have this way taken a hundred wickets for Lancashire in twenty-one successive seasons.

After a year, Cardus was allocated a pen name: he was christened 'Cricketer' by Crozier's redoubtable secretary Madeline Linford, the *Guardian's* only female member of staff, shortly to become its first women's page editor. Was it used advisedly? Because the whole point of 'Cricketer' was that he was not, or barely. He had ceased to play even humbly; he would lead instead a movement of journalists distinguished by their professional writing rather than their amateur cricket credentials. Cricket's most popular pre-war bylines had read like the batting order of the Gentlemen: Ranji, Fry, MacLaren, Jessop, Warner. Between the wars would emerge a new mandarinate: the likes of Harry Altham, Beau Vincent, William Pollock, Harry Carson, R. C. Robertson-Glasgow, and the Great Panjandrum himself, E. W. Swanton. None was so well known as Cardus. In the front row at Old Trafford by now, he was regarded reverently by Robertson-Glasgow:

Here sat Neville Cardus, of the *Manchester Guardian*, slim, grey, contained; master of the rhapsodical style, cutting his epigrams from the most amorphous material ... On the great moments and the top cricketers, he has no equal. He is made for the mountain top, and he ranks among the English essayists.

In this centenary of Cardus's debut as a cricket writer, he still is. For those who have read him before, this book will be a pleasant reminder; for those who have not, it's high time. How to describe Jack Hobbs in the nets? Cardus finds a way, bridging the technical and impressionistic. How to bring alive long-forgotten stumper William Worsley or the batting polymath C. B. Fry? Wodehouse penned nothing funnier. A photograph of Walter Hammond at slip is flavoursome, but Cardus describes *how* he moved.

> His shoulders were broad; the physical frame as a whole maybe at first hinted of top-heaviness somewhere, and there seemed a tendency of his legs, as he stood in the slips, to go together at the knees. At the first sight of a snick from the edge of the bat his energy apparently electrified the shape and substance of him, he became light and boneless, and down to the earth he would dive, all curves and balance, and he would catch a ghost of a 'chance' as if by instinct.

Statistics are dandy, but 216 wickets at 24 explains *who* Clarrie Grimmett was far less effectively than this:

> He walks about the field on dainty feet which step as though with the soft fastidiousness of a cat treading a wet pavement. He is a master of surreptitious arts . . . To play forward to Grimmett, to miss the spin, and then

to find yourself stumped by Oldfield – why, it is like an amputation done under an anaesthetic.

Is he the greatest cricket writer of all? That's a call for those who want to turn literature into listicles. What I would propose is that there's scarcely been a cricket writer so influential – in emancipating his trade from the yoke of the action, in breaking the by-line thrall of the ex-player, and in aspiring to craft work *worth reading*, which is, after all, what we in journalism are trying to do.

Gideon Haigh
Melbourne
May 2019

Myself When Young

To this day I can't explain why one morning in June 1899 I went to Old Trafford for the first time to watch Lancashire. I wasn't a cricketer yet, wasn't much advanced beyond my ninth birthday, and my pocket money seldom ran to twopence a week. It remains, and apparently must remain, a mystery not only what was the attraction that drew me on football that way (and long before the summer holidays had begun); but where did the gate-money come from?

Lancashire were playing Gloucestershire, and as I passed through the turnstiles I heard a terrific roar and didn't know, till I was told by one of the spectators, that Board had just appealed for a catch at the wicket. I am unable to remember if I then knew much about the laws and procedure of the game. I have looked up this match in *Wisden*. Jessop played and made 28 on the day I was present, but he left no indelible impression on this occasion. Why do we retain in memory some things and not others? C.

L. Townsend made 91, and I can vaguely see him now, tall when the ball was coming to him, but he bent gracefully over it as he played forward. F. H. B. Champain drove several fours that made me, with the boy's naïve delight in a play on words, see something very apt in his name.

A year afterwards I was definitely enslaved by cricket for life. On Whit-Monday 1900 I was again at Old Trafford, up at the crack of dawn to get a front seat. For some reason I cannot fathom, Lancashire didn't play Yorkshire that year on Whit Monday; they played Kent. At noon Kent went in first, C. Burnup and Alec Hearne the opening batsmen. I sat facing the pavilion, on the grass in front of the sixpenny seats, which were occupied mainly by men and youths in bowler hats or straw 'cadies'. Moustaches everywhere, and scarcely a girl or woman, though away on the right there was the Ladies' Pavilion, arrayed in long skirts and puffed sleeves. Only women of the middle and upper classes attended cricket matches half a century ago.

From the Stretford end Mold bowled very fast, taking a short run, just three or four strides. At the other end Briggs bowled slow. A fast and a slow bowler to begin, new ball despite. There wouldn't be another new ball during the Kent innings, even if it lasted until tomorrow, which it did. A new ball was available in those times only at the beginning of an innings, as John Gunn once said, 'till t'owd un coom in two'. Mold's speed made sudden havoc of Kent's innings: three wickets went for 11: Hearne, B. D. Bannon, W. H. Patterson. The crowd gloated. I gloated. A marvellous

Bank Holiday morning . . . J. R. Mason came in third wicket down, and to my dismay he seemed to 'see' Mold's bowling at once, which I thought an impossibility. Meanwhile, at the other end of the wicket was this little Burnup man. I didn't like the look of him, for he played everything in the middle of his bat, and nothing flurried him. Burn-up, I said to myself: a silly name.

Mason, thank goodness, was out soon after lunch; but the 'bad start' had been retrieved, and he made 68. The batsman answered to the name of Perkins – T. N. Perkins – another ridiculous name, I assured myself. He missed his stroke at Mold on the off-side time after time. The crowd laughed derision at his helplessness. I joined it. Again I was cheated and cast down. Perkins began to drive classically through covers, as I see it now, left-leg forward. Such cricket today, against very fast bowling, in a searching situation, would be anachronistic. And the little man, Burnup, stayed there, unobtrusive but not idle, gathering runs by neat cuts.

So the warm afternoon went to cool evening. There was no tea interval: drinks were brought into the field, and the crowd rose and stretched itself. T. N. Perkins was not dismissed until he had scored 88; he and Burnup increased Kent's total from 110 for four to 350 for five. If I am not mistaken, Burnup was caught at the wicket from the last over of the day – Kent 400 for six at 'close', Burnup 'c Smith, b Cuttell, 200'. A report of the match in one of the newspapers next day praised Burnup's innings something like this : '... occupied the crease all day ... punctuated by judicious cutting ... periods of slow scoring excusable in view of Kent's bad start ...' A score of 200, after 11 for 3, wouldn't seem inordinately slow nowadays, even with Compton 'occupying' the crease.

I walked home from Old Trafford on the evening of this Whitsun Monday of 1900, a sad cast-down Lancashire boy. Why had Mold allowed that Perkins to survive? All the way from the county ground – planted in the country then, next to the village of Stretford – I walked to Moss Side, down Shrewsbury Street, past Brooks' Bar. Next day I was again at Old Trafford early and I received compensation for the ruined Bank Holiday. I saw Johnny Briggs score 50 – flicking his bat to the off-side in a way which in contemporary circles would quickly bring him to the notice of courts-martial; also he often blocked a ball and dashed out of his ground, pretending to run, 'chancing it', to use the gamester language of the period. He bounced about the wicket as though uncontrolled and uncontrollable.

It was during this summer of 1900, I think, that I saw Johnny Briggs take all ten wickets for Lancashire against Worcestershire at Old Trafford, on a quiet, dull morning. After the fall of the ninth wicket, Arthur Mold pitched his bowling wide, so that Johnny could put the finishing touch to a performance of some distinction half a century ago. For ten minutes he couldn't find any length or direction at all; he was so worked up, so excited, eager, happy, and so afraid this last wicket might elude him after all.

Poor Briggs, it was necessary to send him to an asylum; yet need we be sorry for him? I am assured that during his incarceration he was bowling Australia out every day, and driving four after four through the covers. One of his attendants told me that he'd go into his patient's room to find him beaming, a little exhausted. 'Eight for 52', he would report, recover his breath, 'bring me 'alf a pint, George.'

Briggs wasn't born in Lancashire, he was from Nottinghamshire, and Lockwood too; nor was Arthur Mold a Lancashire man; he belonged to Northamptonshire. But Briggs and Mold became household words in Lancashire, part of the rubric of the day-to-day and evening-by-evening cricket scores:

b Mold
c & b Briggs ...

and so on through many many innings – 'c & b Briggs' – he was one of the cleverest catchers from his own bowling. I suppose in his dying moments he remembered best of all his comical days in the sun the morning at Sydney in December 1894 when he and Bobby Peel caused an astonishing collapse of Australia and won the most remarkable victory in the annals of Test cricket up to that moment. Australia batted first and amassed – for those days of moderate scores 'amassed' is the word – 586. England responded with 325; the follow-on then was automatic;

the fielding side had no option but to field again. So the Australians, tired from long labours under the sun, naturally waxed and waned in attack; England in their second innings scored 437, leaving Australia 177 to win. At the fall of the fifth afternoon, there was no suggestion that the match wouldn't after all go to its expected end, a heavy defeat of England. The wicket was still excellent and Australia made at close 130 or so for two; only a handful to get in the morning, with an array of superb batsmen in hand.

But there was, in the early hours of 20 December, a violent thunderstorm in Sydney, with torrents of tropical rain. It so happened that neither Johnny Briggs nor Bobby Peel heard the thunder or the bursting of the floodgates. They slept well, having drunk deep. The morning was a blaze of sunshine from a clear sky. The earth sprouted green and was dry, Briggs and Feel went to the ground together, blue serge and watch-chains. They went straight into the 'middle', according to a lifetime's habit, to 'look at pitch'. Bobby bent down, with a curious glint in his eye at Briggs. He pressed the earth, then said, 'Eh, Johnny, but soombody's bin wa-aterin' this wicket in t'neight. Coom on – we'll bowl 'em all out in a jiffy' ('bowl' pronounced to rhyme with howl).

And 'bowl' them out they did: Australia collapsed for 166 and England won by ten runs against Australia's first innings total, a record in 1894, of 586.

Other shadowy pictures from the 1900s chase one

another across the film of my mind, perhaps mingling together and eluding pursuit: I saw Carpenter of Essex, also at Whitsun, caught by Tyldesley at deep long-on in front of the Ladies' Pavilion at Old Trafford, the same gracious, black-and-white gabled Ladies' Pavilion where Kenneth Hutching fielded at third-man, tawny, supple, muscular and leonine, the cynosure of all eyes. Carpenter, entirely forgotten now, was a splendid batsman, equalled in stroke-play by not more than half a dozen players of 1950.

In 1901 the wicket at Old Trafford was a scandal. Fast bowling on it imperilled kneecap, breastbone and Adam's apple alike. Something had gone wrong with the ground staff's cultivation of the turf in the early spring. I have been told – but it is too good to be true—that one of the groundsmen was at work 'in the middle', separating with a riddle the impure from the pure and essential marl; he had almost finished the task, and had made two piles of the stuff – but at this critical juncture it was time for midday refreshment.

As luck would have it, he met an old friend at the adjacent inn, where every day he relished a modest sandwich and a glass of ale; on this occasion a reunion after long separation needed to be celebrated. When the groundsman returned to the 'middle' at Old Trafford he proceeded to sow the wrong pile of marl – containing many rough and foreign bodies – into the wicket, a natural enough error, all things considered. As I say, Old Trafford was indeed unfriendly to batsmen that year and a fast bowler's joy and inspiration. I saw C. J. Kortright knock Johnny Tyldesley out of action for an hour or two; but Johnny returned after lunch, his forehead bandaged, and he counter-attacked the fastest bowler of all time.

I am not sure that wasn't in this same match against Essex, in the early 1900s, that Tyldesley didn't win a match in an over. Seven or eight Lancashire wickets were down and nearly twenty runs still wanted when a storm broke; for an hour black clouds had rumbled up. Suddenly great spots of rain fell; you could hear the smack of them on the grass; then a flash of lightning was seen across the Stretford sky. Tyldesley, quicker than the storm, hit four fours in one over from Buckenham; square-cuts, flicks high over the slips, death-and-glory strokes as forked as the lightning. Before the players could reach the shelter of the pavilion, Trafford was a lake or an archipelago. In this season of dangerous pitches C. B. Fry one day extracted some pebbles or minerals from the wicket, and they were later exhibited in the window of Tyldesley's cricket outfit shop in Deansgate. People would look at them for hours, like students going the rounds of a museum of geology.

This same season, playing half his innings on this nasty, brutish turf, Tyldesley scored more than 3,000 runs, average more than fifty, which must remain one of the wonders of batsmanship. Consider, too, the pleasure he gave while making 3,000, to himself as much as anybody.

By the time 1904 burgeoned for Lancashire cricket, I

was an addict, hanging on to every hour's news from every-where, Taunton to Trent, Bournemouth to Bradford. In 1904 Lancashire won the county championship and didn't lose a match; and the first three in Lancashire's batting order have never been equalled by any other first three, for mingled majesty, grace, swordlike power and brilliance: Maclaren, Spooner, Tyldesley.

Of Maclaren I can say no more: I have written of him elsewhere. Nobody has occupied a batting crease with his sovereignty, his sense of born prerogative. A youthful impression of him will not fade — yet I can't believe it is a true one. On the other hand, I am not poet enough ever to have 'invented' a picture as evocative and as true to the Maclarenesque manner and atmosphere as this:

On a calm morning at Old Trafford in that distant and indeed lost world of the early 1900s, Maclaren went forth with Albert Ward to open the Lancashire innings against Warwickshire. Hargreave, a clever slow left-hander, began the attack, and in his first over Maclaren played forward with the sweep of grandeur which was for him sign of the blood-royal; but Hargreave's ball, 'coming with the arm', beat Maclaren and bowled him. Only the leg bail fell. And when Maclaren returned to the pavilion the members rose for him in silence, as he passed them up the steps. At least, if they didn't, they should have.

Batsmanship of Manners

In the summer of 1899 a schoolboy walked to the wicket at Lord's to begin a Lancashire innings against Middlesex; with him was Albert Ward. He was a graceful young cricketer, and a little tuft of hair stood up on the crown of his head. His flannels seemed soft and billowy. This boy – his name R. H. Spooner –was making his first appearance in county cricket in his summer holidays, fresh from Marlborough. It would be hard to imagine a severer ordeal for anybody: a trial in the sacrosanct air of Lord's, the searching eyes of the pavilion on you, MacLaren your captain, and one of the bowlers against you Albert Trott at his best, spinning and curving and dipping the ball astonishingly.

R. H. Spooner that day made 83, an innings full of strokes that seemed to ripple over the grass, light and lovely as sunshine. Straight from the playing fields of Marlborough he came and conquered – nay, the word conquered is too hard and aggressive for Spooner: he charmed and won our heart and the hearts of all his opponents. 'It were a pleasure to bowl to Maister Spooner,' said an old player to me the other day; 'his batting were as nice as he were hisself.' Yes, it was nice; it was the batsmanship of manners. Spooner told us in every one of his drives past cover that he did not come from the hinterland of Lancashire, where cobbled streets sound with the noise of clogs and industry; he played always as though on the elegant lawns of Aigburth; his cricket was 'county' in the social sense of the term. This flavour of equability took the grimness out of a Lancashire and Yorkshire match even: I once saw him score 200 against Hirst, Rhodes, and Haigh at Bank Holiday time, and he transformed Old Trafford to Canterbury. I'll swear that on that day long ago there were tents and bunting in the breeze of Manchester while Spooner bat flicked and flashed from morning till evening.

He was the most lyrical of cricketers, and for that reason he had no need to play a long innings to tell us his secret. The only difference between 30 by Spooner and 150 was a matter of external and unessential form or duration; the spirit moved from the very beginning. A rondo by Mozart is just as complete and true as a symphony by him. One daffodil is as precious and delectable as a hundred daffodils. And a single stroke by Spooner was likewise a quality absolute, beyond the need of mensuration or any mathematical means of valuation whatever. If you consider

Spooner's average for the whole of his career it will tell you nothing of consequence about his cricket; as well count the word in a poem or the notes in an allegro.

I must suppose that he hit the ball hard, because I remember seeing fieldsmen blowing their hands after they had stopped a stroke by Spooner. And once I saw on the shilling side when Parker, of Gloucestershire, bowled his first ball in county cricket: Spooner pulled it clean over the rails, and it crashed amongst the dust and cinders like an exploding shell. Yet my impression today is that Spooner's cricket was all bouquet; I think of it I think of a rose, because of the perfume, not because of the substantial stuff which went to its making. Never did I see Spooner strike an ugly position, either at the wicket or in the field, where at cover he was the picture of swift, diving elegance.

If I have called his batsmanship that of manners, I do not mean it was ever affected: every innings by Spooner was natural and modest, like the man himself. The poise was a consequence of an instinctive balance of cultured technical parts. What's bred in the bone comes out in an innings; I never saw Spooner bat without seeing, as a background for his skill and beauty, the fields of Marlborough, and all the quiet summertime amenities of school cricket. He was my favourite player when I was a boy – he and Victor Trumper. And with a boy's illogicality I at one and the same time thought him wonderful and yet always in need of my prayers. All the time I watched him – and often I played truant to do so – I said in my heart, 'Please, Lord, don't let Reggie get out; let him score a century.' Sometimes I was more moderate: 'Please, Lord, let Reggie make 59.' I called him 'Reggie' even in my petitions to Providence. Like every delightful cricketer, he seemed at any moment ready to get out; no great batsman has ever been content to keep strictly within the scope of the things that can be done safely. I remember once seeing Spooner begin an innings against Hirst. All round his legs was the notorious Hirst 'trap' – four fieldsmen holding out avaricious hands. And Hirst swerved the ball terrifically across from Spooner's off-stump. And time after time did Spooner flick the swinging ball at his wrists' end through the leg-trap – each stroke a brave and lovely butterfly going into the flame.

Yet he was a sound as well as a brilliant batsman. There is a stupid legend about the batsmen of old. Because they made runs handsomely it is thought in certain places that they were constantly thrusting out the left leg and leaving their stumps exposed to the breaking ball. Not long ago a cricketer actually said to me, 'Yes, Spooner was splendid to watch, but he couldn't abide the "googly".'

And I said, 'God forgive you for blasphemy.'

In 1912 Spooner made a century against South Africa and amongst the bowlers were Pegler, Faulkner and Schwarz. These men have never had superiors as master of the 'googly': they were as clever at spinning the ball as anybody today. Spooner played them easefully – with his bat, not with his pads. He was superb in his back strokes: he could hit a four from a defensive position. The second line of defence – which is the pads – was known well enough to the batsmen of the Golden Age: Arthur Shrewsbury organised it scientifically. But it was a second and not a first line of defence; Spooner never put his bat ignominiously over his shoulder to any ball and stuck out his legs crudely and ungraciously. The fact that he could achieve a great innings as a boy against Albert Trott is ample retort to the absurd notion that he was ever at a loss against swerve or spin. No bowler who ever lived could give to a cricket ball more than Trott's curve and break.

Spooner and MacLaren – has a county possessed two batsmen who could begin an innings with more than their appeal to the imagination? They were as the King and the Prince, or as the eagle and the flashing swallow. Spooner was one of the cricketers who, when I was very young, made me fall in love with the game; I think of his batting now, in middle age, with gratitude. The delight of it all went into my mind, I hope, to stay there, with all the delight that life has given me in various shapes, aspects, and essences. When the form has gone –for it is material and accidental, and therefore perishable – the spirit remains. And Spooner's cricket in spirit was kin with sweet music, and the wind that makes long grasses wave, and the singing of Elisabeth Schumann in Johann Strauss, and the poetry of Herrick. Why do we deny the art of a cricketer, and rank it lower than a vocalist's or a fiddler's? If anybody tells me that R. H. Spooner did not compel a pleasure as aesthetic as any compelled by the most celebrated Italian tenor that ever lived I will write him down a purist and an ass.

By Three Runs

The most thrilling finish of all the Test matches ever fought at Old Trafford happened on the Saturday afternoon of 26 July 1902. It was the decisive game of the rubber, and Australia won it by three runs, snatching the spoils from the lion's mouth. The match at the end seemed to get right out of the control of the men that were making it; it seemed to take on a being of its own, a volition of its own, and the mightiest cricketers in the land looked as though they were in the grip of a power of which they could feel the presence but whose ends they could not understand. As events rushed them to crisis even Maclaren, Ranjitsinhji, Trumper, Noble, and Darling – most regal of cricketers – could only utter: 'Here we do but as we may; no further dare.' The game, in Kipling's term, was more than the player of the game.

The match was designed, surely, by the gods for their

sport. Even the victors were abominably scourged. On the second day, when the issue was anybody's, Darling played an innings which, as things turned out, must be said to have won Australia's laurels as much as anything else. Australia in their second innings had lost 3 wickets – those of Trumper, Duff, and Hill – for 10 runs and now possessed an advantage worth no more than 47. Under a sky of rags, the fitful and sinister sunlight coming through, Darling let all his superb might go at the English attack. His hitting had not the joyfulness of mastership in it; its note was desperation. He plainly felt the coils of circumstance about him; he plainly was aware of the demon of conflict that had the game in grip. And the defiant action of his bat was like a fist shaken at the unfriendly heavens.

It was in this innings of Darling's that the gods played their first cruel trick. For with Darling's score only 17 he was impelled to sky a ball to the deep field a high but easy catch. And who was the wight that the ironic powers had decreed should shoulder the responsibility of taking that crucial catch? His name was Tate – Tate of Sussex, a kindly fellow who never did harm to a soul. The humour of the gods really began when this cricketer was asked to play for England instead of George Hirst. Tate was a capital bowler, but as soon as he was seen in the company of the great the question went out: 'What is he doing in this galley?' Tate had not the stern fibre of character that can survive in an air of high tragedy; his bent was for pastoral comedy down at Horsham. Tate missed the catch, and never looked like holding it. As he stood under the ball, which hung for a while in the air – an eternity to Tate – and then dropped like a stone, his face turned white. Darling survived to make 37 out of a total of 86.

Had Tate held the catch Australia could hardly have got a score of more than 50, for Lockwood and Rhodes, that Friday afternoon, bowled magnificently. Yet when Tate laid himself down to rest in the evening, can he not be imagined as saying to himself: 'Well, it's nearly all over now, and as far as Tate of Sussex is concerned, the worst must have happened. I never *asked t*o play for England – they thrust greatness on me – and I'll be well out of it this time tomorrow, back to Brighton, and who'll remember my missed catch after a week? What's a muff in the field in a cricketer's career – everybody makes them.' If Tate did console his spirit in this way the poor man did not know he was born. The gods had not finished with him; the next day he was to be put on the rack and have coals of fire heaped on his head.

On the Saturday England were left with 124 to get for victory. A tiny score with the cream of batsmanship at hand. But there had been five hours of rain in the night, and Trumble and Saunders were bowling for Australia. Still, England seemed nicely placed at lunch; the total 36 for none and Maclaren and Palairet undefeated. The crowd took its sustenance light-heartedly; everybody lived at ease in a fool's paradise as rosily lighted as Tate's. Here, again, was the humorous touch of the gods: men that are taken suddenly out of contentment are the more likely to writhe in Gehenna. After lunch the sun got to work on the wicket, and straightway Palairet was bowled by an intolerable break from Saunders. Tyldesley came in, and, with Maclaren, the game was forced.

The play of these two batsmen gave the crowd the first hint that all was not yet settled in England's favour, for it was the play of cricketers driven to desperate remedies. The runs, they seemed to say, can only be got if we hurry; there's the sun as well as Trumble and Saunders to frustrate. Tyldesley jumped to the bowling; he hit 16 runs in quick time before he was caught in the slips.

England 68 for 2 – 56 wanted now. And, said the crowd, not yet sniffing the evil in the wind, *only* 56, with Ranji, Abel, Jackson, Braund, and Lilley to come, to say nothing of Rhodes and Lockwood. Why, the game is England's!

Four runs after Tyldesley's downfall Maclaren was caught by Duff in the long field. An indiscreet stroke, yet whose was the right to blame the man for making it? It had come off time after time during his priceless innings of 35, and England could not afford to throw a single possible run away. Maclaren had played like a gambler at a table – not looking as though he were making runs, but rather as one who had ample boundaries at his bat's end to bank on every throw of the dice.

Abel and Ranji were in when at last the multitude unmistakably saw the evil day face to face. For what sort of a Ranji was this? Palsy was on him. You could have sworn that he shook at the knees. It looked like Ranji: his shirt rippled in the wind even as it did on that day at Old Trafford six years earlier than this, the day on which he conjured 154 runs out of the Australians. Yes, it looked like Ranji – the same slight body, the same inscrutable, bland face. Alas! the spirit had gone – here was a deserted shrine. Thousands of eyes turned away from Ranji and looked to Abel for succour. Ah, this is better – the pertness of little Abel lightened the soul. He made gallant runs – a boundary over Hill's head. 'Cheeky' work this – batsmanship with *gaminerie*. 'Bravo, Bobby!' shouted the Old Trafford crowd. At 92 Ranji was out, leg-before-wicket to Trumble. Well, the sophist crowd told itself, that was bound to happen; he never looked good for any at all. But 5 runs more and Trumble bowled Abel. England 97 for 5 – 27 needed.

'It's quite all right,' said a parson on the half-crown stand; 'there's really no cause for anxiety. To doubt the ability of Jackson, Braund, Lilley, Lockwood, and Rhodes to get a paltry 27 runs would be scandalous. Besides, I do believe that fellow Tate is a batsman – he has an average of 16 for Sussex.' The century went up with cheers to herald it – the crowd made as much of joyful noise as it could, presumably in the hope that cheering would put a better face on the scoring-board. Jackson, who made a century in the first innings, scored 7 in his best 'Parliamentary' manner – neat, politic runs. Then he was caught by Gregory, and now the cat was indeed out of the bag; sophistry passed away from the heaped-up ranks. 'Who'd 'a' thowt it?' said a man on the sixpenny side. Who, indeed? At that very moment of agony at Old Trafford, people far away in the city read in the latest editions, 'England 92 for 3', and agreed that it wasn't worth the journey to Old Trafford, that it had been a good match, that the Australians were fine sportsmen, and jolly good losers.

Sixteen runs – four good boundaries or four bad ones – would bring the game into England's keeping when Lilley reached the wicket.

He was frankly and unashamedly in some slight panic. He hit out impetuously, as who should say: 'For the Lord's sake let it be settled and done with quickly.' Braund was overthrown at 109, and Lockwood made not a run. Lilley lashed his bat about like a man distraught. Rhodes is his companion now, and stands on guard ever so cool. Eight runs will do it, and 'There goes four of them!' affirms the red-hot crowd as Lilley accomplishes a grand drive into the deep.

'Well hit, sir!' shouts our parson. 'Nothing like taking your courage in both hands against these Australian fellows. Well hit, sir!'

Clem Hill is seen running along the boundary's edge as though the fiend were after him. Trying to save the four, is he? – even from as certain a boundary hit as this! Extraordinary men, Australians; never give anything away. Hill, in fact, saved the boundary in the most decisive manner in the world by holding the ball one-handed before it pitched. The impetus of his run carried him 20 yards beyond the place where he made the catch – a catch which put incredulity into the face of every man and woman at Old Trafford that day. 'A sinful catch,' said the parson.

Tate, the last man in, watched Rhodes ward off three balls from Trumble, and then rain stopped play. Yes, rain stopped play for 40 minutes – and England eight runs short of triumph with the last men in. But though it was heavy rain there was always a bright sky not far away – another piece of subtle torture by the gods, for nobody could think that the weather was going to put an end to the afternoon. It would clear up all right in time; the agony had to be gone through.

The crowd sat around the empty field, waiting, but hardly daring to hope. The tension was severe. Yet surely there were calm minds here and there. Why, under a covered stand sat two old gentlemen who were obviously *quite* indifferent to the issue. One was actually reading to the other the leading article from one of the morning papers. Moreover, he was reading it in a controlled and deliberately articulated voice. '"Sir M. Hicks-Beach argued yesterday,"' he read, '"that even if Ireland was overtaxed in 1894, its grievance was less today, because taxation had not increased quite so rapidly in Ireland as in the United Kingdom."' And the other old gentleman, so far was he from troubling his head needlessly over a mere cricket match, promptly took up the points in the argument, and he too spoke in a perfectly controlled and deliberately articulated voice. 'Two wrongs,' he commented, 'do not make a right.' Excited about England and Australia? Not a bit of it, sir! We trust we are old and sensible enough to put a correct valuation on a game of cricket.

In the pavilion Tate was dying a thousand deaths. All depended on him – Rhodes was safe enough. In his head, maybe, notions went round and round like a wheel. 'You've only to keep your bat straight,' he might well have said to himself time after time. 'Don't even move it from the block hole. I've heard tell if you keep your bat quite still it's a thousand to one against any ball hitting the wicket.' . . .

At six minutes to five the Australians went into action again. Saunders bowled at Tate – a fast one. Tate saw something hit the ground and he made a reflex action at it. Click! Tate looked wildly around him. What had happened? A noise came to him over the wet grass, sounding like a distant sea. The crowd was cheering; he had snicked a boundary. Another snick like that and the game is England's and Tate safe for posterity! The ball was returned from the ring, and Darling slightly but impressively rearranged his field, the while Saunders bent down to a sawdust heap. Bloodless, calculating Australians they were.

Tate got himself down on his bat once more, and the wheel in his poor head went round faster and faster. ' . . . Bat straight . . . don't move . . . can't hit wicket . . . block-hole . . . don't move. . . . Bat straight . . . can't hit wicket . . .' And the gods fooled him to the top of his bent – to the last. Saunders's fourth ball was not only good enough for Tate's frail bat; it was good enough for the best bat in England. It was fast through the air and – it was a shooter. It broke Tate's wicket, and, no doubt, broke Tate's heart and the heart of the crowd.

In 20 minutes Old Trafford was deserted save for one or two groundsmen who tended to the battlefield. The figures on the scoreboard had revolved, obliterating all records of the match from the face of it, which now looked vacantly over the grass. The gods had finished their sport – finished even with Tate. Yet not quite. A week later, on the Saturday afternoon following this, Tate met the Australians again in his beloved Sussex, and he was graciously permitted to play an innings of 22 not out against them – and a capital innings at that.

Bill Worsley, Straight from the Pits

Bill Worsley belonged to the hinterland of the county where existence is carried on near to the knuckle, where cobbled streets go up and down hill, where in the pitch-black of cold winter mornings mills' sirens or 'buzzers' awakened the dead, and the rattle of clogs was like the sound of a sort of Last Day or Resurrection. From one of the pits of Lancashire emerged this Bill Worsley, who kept wicket for the county in the great high noon of Maclaren's reign.

He got his chance unexpectedly. The Lancashire Eleven was touring the West of England and the regular wicket-keeper received an injury to the hand which rendered him a casualty for the rest of the summer. A telegram was sent for reinforcements and was received by Bill Worsley on his back in a seam of a coal-mine. He was brought to the surface, where he blinked his eyes to get accustomed to the light of day. After he had slowly read the telegram he said, without emotion: 'It's signed A. C. Maccle-aren' – he always pronounced it that way – 'and it ses Ah've to pack oop and go to Edgbaston, Birmingham, and keep wickets for Lankysheer.' He scratched his head and added: 'Ah'm non so sure as Ah rightly knows where Edgbaston is.'

But his proud and admiring friends saw him to the train and bought the correct railway ticket, and Bill departed, with a farewell message as he leaned out of the carriage window: "Ah reckon Ah'll be back wi' thee all in a day or two. Look after mi whippets.'

He duly arrived at the cricket ground of Edgbaston. Lancashire were about to play Warwickshire. Bill stripped and sat in a corner in the dressing-room. Nobody spoke to him and he, as he afterwards said, kept himself to 'his-self'. He was discerned by Walter Brearley, the fast bowler and an 'amateur', meaning a 'gentleman'. Brearley, the kindest man and the friendliest in the world, hailed the newcomer. 'You are Worsley, aren't you; wicket-keeper for us today?'

'Yes, sir,' replied Bill.

'Come and have a drink,' said Brearley: 'We'll just have *one*, to baptise your first appearance for the county. This is your opportunity, Bill; just you keep a decent wicket and you can say goodbye to the pit, and have a grand life up and down the country. Come on, Bill – this way!' Brearley led Bill to the bar in the members' enclosure. When they reached the counter, Brearley smote Bill on the back and said: 'Now, Bill; what'll you have to celebrate this famous day in your life?'

'Well,' responded Bill politely, 'if you don't mind, Maister Brearley, Ah'll 'ave a Creem de Month.'

Brearley was rather taken aback. 'A what?' he said.

And Bill repeated with equal politeness: 'A Creem de Month, if you please, Maister Brearley.'

Brearley concealed his astonishment and gave the order, including a can of beer for himself, which he picked up and drained at a draught. 'There's luck to you, Bill,' he gulped.

Whereupon Bill drank his green fluid and said: 'The same to you, Maister Brearley, and many of 'em.'

Lancashire lost the toss, and Maclaren led his team into the field. When he reached the middle he as usual spent some time distributing his forces, waving men here and there, while Brearley measured his run and swung his arms and prepared to attack. The two opening Warwickshire batsmen came to the wicket, and Kinneir took his guard. All was ready.

Then Maclaren at first slip withdrew his attention from the bowler and the precise position to an inch of cover-point: he saw Bill Worsley 'standing up', an inch or so from the stumps. 'Worsley,' he said, 'get back a bit – Mr Brearley happens to be pretty quick.'

'Just as you like, Maister Maccle-aren,' said Bill, retreating exactly four inches.

'Farther back still,' shouted Maclaren impatiently: 'he's fast, I'm telling you.'

'Just as you please, Maister Maccle-aren,' reiterated Bill, retreating another four inches.

To himself Maclaren said: 'Well, if he wants his so-and-so head knocked off, very well.'

The match began. Bill 'stood up' to Brearley. Kinneir, a left hander and a most obstinate batsman on a good wicket, was in form. He scored ten in a quarter of an hour – rapid work for him. Then he moved gently over to the off-side and beautifully glanced at a fine angle to leg. Worsley also moved across, made a brilliant catch and, without a change of action or pause, sent the ball high into the air with a one-handed jerk behind his back.

'What the . . . what the . . .' expostulated Maclaren.

But Brearley said, behind his hand, 'Hush, Archie; you'll put him off! Marvellous catch!'

So Maclaren held his peace and the game was resumed. The next batsman was the formidable W. G. Quaife, most notorious of stone-wallers, almost beyond the powers of known science to get out on a hard wicket under six hours. He, too, began well and he, too, presently moved gently across his wickets and glanced exquisitely off his pads, fine to leg. And again did Worsley swoop on the ball, catch it, and with one comprehensive and encircling action jerk it sky-high behind his back.

This was too much for Maclaren. In spite of Brearley's muffled, 'Shush, Archie; you'll only put him off. Marvellous catch!' – in spite of Brearley's kind admonitions, Maclaren approached Bill. 'Well caught, Worsley,' he said, 'but damn it all, what's the idea of this behind-the-back foolery?'

'Well, Maister Maccle-aren,' replied Bill, 'we allus does

it in t' Saturday afternoon league – a little bit o' 'fluence, tha knows, sir.'

'You can't do it here,' said Maclaren, 'in front of all these people. Bless my soul. Now, Bill, get on with your job. You're doing splendidly. But no more bits o' 'fluence, if you don't mind.'

As it happened, one or two Warwickshire batsmen took root, and Lancashire spent a long day in the field. But Bill acquitted himself well, though he did not get any more chances to make a catch. When they all came to the pavilion at close of play, it was discovered that Bill had been wearing primitive gloves. His hands were swollen and black. A pair of scissors was needed to cut his gloves away from his wounded hands.

Brearley's heart went out to Bill. He took him to the bar, the same bar where at the beginning of the day they had drunk to Bill's first appearance for Lancashire.

'Come, Bill,' said Brearley, 'you've won your colours. You'll come with us on the whole tour now. No more pit for you, my lad. You've done "gradely". But for God's sake, get some proper gloves and drop all that behind-the-back business. Can't do it at Lord's – Heaven help us ... Well, here's to you, Bill. Let's celebrate the occasion properly now. What'll you have?'

And Bill replied, polite as ever: 'Well, if you don't mind, Maister Brearley, Ah'll have a Creem de Month.'

Victor Trumper

When Victor Trumper died he was a young man and a cricketer. The death of a cricketer before age has fallen on him is sad; it is even against nature. Well may he look down on our fields from his chill hall of immortality, far removed from the jolly flesh and blood of this life, and cry out, 'Another day in the sun and wind and I not there, I not there!'

It is only a score or so of years since Victor Trumper played a great innings at Old Trafford in a Test match and hit a century before lunch. Can it be true he is now part of the impersonal dust – this Victor Trumper we knew so well? All the little intimate delights belonging to cricket, a man's flannels and his bat, his own boyish enthusiasm for a summer game – surely these are things which ought to hold a cricketer to the friendly earth till he is tired of them? You can never speak to an Australian about Victor Trumper without seeing his eyes glisten with pride and affection;

Trumper will always remain for your true Australian the greatest batsman that ever lived. But it was in England that Trumper achieved his most wonderful play; every lover of the game will pause for a space in the hurly-burly of the present period's Test matches to spare a moment in which to do homage to Trumper.

> The shadow stayed not, but the splendour stays,
> Our brother, till the last of English days.

In 1902, a season of bowler's wickets here, Trumper's batsmanship was by day of a brilliance that beggared description. Lest this language be thought overdrawn (I am not above suspicion in my use of words when it comes to writing of a Trumper), I will draw on the restrained vocabulary used in the MCC's *Cricket Scores and Biographies*:

> For Trumper the season [of 1902] was one long triumphal progress, and those who were fortunate enough to witness his amazing brilliance will never be able to forget the unrivalled skill and resource he displayed. On sticky wickets he hit with freedom and scored well, often whilst his companions were puddling about the crease, unable to make headway and seemingly content if they could keep up their wickets ... He was always to be feared on Australian wickets, but followers of the game in England were privileged to see him at his zenith.

Was it not genius that made Trumper a master batsman in conditions not common to Australian cricket? Only a few of our own batsmen were resourceful and skilful enough to conquer the English pitch as it was in the old days whenever sunshine and rain got to work on it. Trumper learned his game in the land where perfect grounds are the rule; he came to this country, and in a season that saw the wickets of English batsmen of the highest rank falling like corn before the sickle he was masterful. Trumper in 1902 took our finest spin bowlers by the scruff of the neck, usually from the first ball sent to him, drove them, thrust, glanced and 'carted' them, right and left, for all the world as though they had been schoolboys. Amongst these same bowlers happened to be Rhodes, Taigh, Lockwood, J. T. Hearne, Hirst, Barnes, Trott, Wass and Braund.

In the Test match at Manchester, as I say, Trumper scored a century before lunch; even Maclaren, with all his strategy, could not set the field for him. No shibboleth about an 'outer and inner ring' of fieldsmen ever troubled Victor Trumper. He was master of all the strokes, and he could use almost any one of them at his pleasure, no matter the manner of ball bowled at him. He would cut the identical length which a moment later he would drive. It was, indeed, impossible to pitch a length at all to Trumper on one of his great days. 'He would,' says the sober record of the MCC, 'get a yorker to the square-leg boundary, and it was by no means unusual to see him cut a ball off the middle stump for four. Some of his biggest hits, which went over the ring, were made without any apparent effort.'

Let me give a few more prosaic facts about Trumper before I squander words over his art (whoever would not be spendthrift of language about Trumper, let him not write on him at all). In our bowler's year of 1902, Trumper scored eleven centuries, two against Essex in the same match; he hit a century for Australia at Old Trafford before lunch, as we have seen. In the Test match at Sheffield in 1899 he scored 62 out of 80 in 50 minutes. For New South Wales, on a bowler's pitch, he made 101 out of 139 in 57 minutes, at Sydney in 1905. He scored in Test matches 17,150 runs at an average of 45.01, an astonishing figure for a batsman who lived so dangerously at the wicket. In Australia he averaged 84.30 (for 843 runs) in 1912–13; 72.10 (for 721 runs) in 1899–1900; and 69.22 (for 1,246 runs) in 1910–11. Facts, as Mr Bounderby would say. And now let us come to the imperishable spirit of the man.

To change the old saying about the strawberry, God no doubt could create a better batsman than Victor Trumper if He wished, but so far He hasn't. Ranjitsinhji is the only cricketer that might be instanced as Trumper's like in genius. But even Ranji was not so great a match-winner on all wickets. Even Ranji never smashed the best attack of his day with the sudden vehemence of Trumper. Ranji did not rout his bowlers; he lured them onwards to ruin by the dark, stealthy magic of his play; the poor men were enchanted into futility. Trumper put them to the sword . . .

Yet it was a knightly sword. There never lived a more chivalrous cricketer than Trumper. I see his bat now, in my mind's eye, a banner in the air, streaming its brave runs over the field. He was ready always to take up the challenge of a good ball; Trumper never fell into the miserable philosophy of 'Safety first – wait for the bad ball.'

And what of the man's style? He had, as C. B. Fry put it, no style, yet he was all style. 'His whole bent is aggressive,' wrote Fry, 'and he plays a defensive stroke only as a very last resort.' Imagine Spooner's cover drive, Hirst's pull, Maclaren's hook, J. T. Tyldesley's square cut, Macartney's late cut through the slips – imagine a mingling of all these attributes of five great and wholly different batsmen, and perhaps some notion of Trumper will emerge in your mind. The grand manner of Maclaren, the lyrical grace of Spooner, the lion energy of Jessop, the swift opportunist spirit of Tyldesley – all these excellencies were compounded proportionately in Trumper. Do I exaggerate youthful impressions of the man? Then let me give here a tribute to Trumper uttered to me by an English cricketer whose name stands for all that is masterful and majestic in our batsmanship: 'In comparison with an innings by Victor at his best, my best was shoddy – hackwork!'

Trumper's winged batsmanship was seen in the golden age of cricket; he was, at his finest, master of some of the greatest bowlers the game has ever known. When he played for Australia, Clem Hill, Noble, Duff, Darling, S. E. Gregory, and Armstrong were batsmen with him.

Splendid as the cricket of these men might be, day after day, whenever Trumper got out the light seemed to go for a while from an Australian innings. 'The eagle is gone, and now crows and daws.' We make an artist's immortality by thinking upon and loving his work; Trumper was an artist-cricketer; let him live again in the mouths of men whenever Test matches are in action. Since he accomplished some of his greatest innings in this land, English cricket owes much to his ghost.

Ranjitsinhji

Cricketers will never see the like of Ranjitsinhji; he was entirely original, and there is nothing in all the history and development of batsmanship with which we can compare him. His style was a remarkable instance of the way a man can express personal genius in a game — nay, not only a personal genius but the genius of a whole race. For Ranjitsinhji's cricket was of his own country; when he batted a strange light was seen for the first time on English fields, a light out of the East. It was lovely magic and not prepared for by anything that had happened in cricket before Ranji came to us.

In the 'nineties the game was absolutely English: it was even Victorian. W. G. Grace for years had stamped on cricket the English mark and the mark of the period. It was the age of simple first principles, of the stout respectability of straight bat and good-length ball; the flavours everywhere were John Bull's. And then suddenly this visitation of dusky, supple legerdemain happened; a man was seen playing cricket as nobody born in England could possibly have played it. The honest length ball was not met by the honest straight bat, but there was a flick of the wrist, and lo! the straight ball was charmed away to the leg boundary. And nobody quite saw or understood how it all happened. Bowler stood transfixed, and possibly they crossed themselves. I once asked Ted Wainwright, the Yorkshire cricketer, what he thought of Ranji, and Wainwright said, 'Ranji, he never made a Christian stroke in his life.' Why should he have done? The style is the man, and Ranji belonged to the land of Hazlitt's Indian jugglers, where beauty is subtle and not plain and unambiguous.

Marvellous game of cricket that can give us a W. G. Grace, English as a Gloucestershire tree, and George Hirst, Yorkshire as a broad moor, and Ranji as true to his racial psychology as any of them!

The game has known no greater spectacle than that of C. B. Fry and Ranji as they made a great stand for Sussex. I notice that Mr. J. A. Spender has described the Ranji-Fry combination as 'the perfect display of the first-wicket stand'. But Ranji never went in first with Fry; he always batted second wicket down, and thereby hangs a tale – and again the teller of it is Ted Wainwright. 'Ranji and Fry', he would murmur as memory moved in him, 'every year it were the same owd story. We used to go down to Brighton with the sun shining and the ground hard as iron. And Sussex allus won the toss. And we all went on the field and started bowlin', and, sure enough, we'd get Vine out and the score board would say Sussex 20 for 1. And then George Hirst would get Killick out quick, and we all on us said, "Come on, Yorkshire, we're going grand; Sussex 31 for 2!!"' Wainwright paused here in his narrative, and after a while he added, 'But, bless you, we knowed there were nowt in it. Close of play, Sussex three 'undred and ninety for two, and the same owd tale every year.'

Bowlers have never known a problem so heartbreaking as the problem of Fry and Ranji on a perfect Brighton wicket. Happy the man who today can close his eyes and see again the vision of Ranji, his rippling shirt of silk, his bat like a yielding cane making swift movements which circled round those incomparable wrists. He saw the ball quicker than any other batsman; he made his strokes later, so late, indeed, that Lockwood almost saw his great breakback crashing on the leg stump while Ranji remained there at his crease, apparently immobile. Then, at the last fraction of the last second, Ranji's body leaned gently over his front leg, the bat glinted in the sun, and we saw Lockwood throw up his hands to heaven as the ball went to the boundary, exquisitely fine to leg, with the speed of thought. This leg glance was Ranji's own stroke, but it is a mistake to say he could not drive. Usually he was too indolent for forcible methods, but none the less his front-of-the-wicket play could reach unparalleled range and precision; and his cut was a dazzling lance of batsmanship.

He caused a revolution in the game: he demonstrated

the folly of the old lunge forward to a ball seductive in length. Ranji's principle was to play back or to drive, and his many imitators contrived in the course of years to evolve the hateful two-eyed stance from Ranji's art, which, of course, was not for ordinary mortals to imitate. He is today a legend. Modern lovers of the game, jealous of their own heroes, will no doubt tell us that Ranji, like all the old masters, was a creation of our fancy in a world old-fashioned and young. We who saw him will keep silence as the sceptics commit their blasphemy. We have seen what we have seen. We can feel the spell yet, we can go back in our minds to hot days in an England of forgotten peace and plenty, days when Ranji did not so much bat for us as enchant us, bowlers and all, in a way all his own, so that when at last he got out we were as though suddenly wakened from a dream. It was more than a cricketer and more than a game that did it for us.

The Greatest Test Match

On a bright day in the spring of 1921 I went to Lord's, hoping to see the first practice of the Australians. But the place was deserted, save for the man at the gates. He told me Armstrong's men were being entertained that afternoon somewhere in the City, and that they wouldn't be in the nets till after tea. Still, he added, with a touch of human nature not too common at Lord's, if I liked I could enter the ground and sit and enjoy myself in the sun till they came.

I sat on a bench with my feet spread out so that they touched the soft grass. A great calm was over the field. The trees beyond the Nursery were delicate with fresh green, and the fine old pavilion seemed to nod in the sunshine. It was an occasion for a reverie, and I fell to affectionate thoughts upon the great days of cricket, of the history that had been made on the field which stretched before me. I thought of Grace, of Spofforth, of Hornby, of A. G. Steel ... Maybe I dozed for a while.

Then I was conscious of a voice. 'Would you mind moving up a little? This seat is rather congested.'

I looked around and saw sitting by my side a man in a tight black coat which buttoned high on his chest. He had sidewhiskers and wore a low turned-down collar and a high bowler hat. A handkerchief was showing from a breast pocket in his jacket. Not quite awake yet, I moved up.

'Thank you,' he said. 'I'm sorry I disturbed you. A nap carries one comfortably through a long wait at these matches. What a crowd there is!'

I looked round. I was in the middle of a big crowd indeed. In front of me sat a parson. He was reading *The Times*. I glanced over his shoulder and saw the headline: 'Egyptian Campaign: Sir G. Wolseley's Dispatch.'

The man at my side said, 'Were you here yesterday, sir?' and before I could reply he added, 'It was a considerable day's cricket, and the *Post* has an excellent account. Perhaps you've seen it?' He handed me a copy of the *Morning Post*, and, thanking him, I took it. The paper was dated 29 August 1882. In a column headed 'England v Australia' I read that on the day before, Australia had been dismissed for 63 by Barlow and Peate, and that England, captained by A. N. Hornby, had made in reply 101. Then I understood my situation. And what is more I now understood it without the slightest astonishment. Even the aspect of the ground, which told me it was Kennington Oval and not Lord's, did not embarrass me. It was enough that I was one of the crowd that was to witness the second

day's cricket in the ninth Test match — the most famous
Test match of all.

I gave the *Post* back to my companion in silence. 'A considerable day's cricket indeed, sir,' said the parson. 'But
England ought to have made more runs. Our batting was
distinctly mediocre — almost as bad as the Australians'.'
A loud cheer disturbed his argument. Down the pavilion
steps walked the England Eleven in single file, led by
Hornby. With him was WG, and he passed along the field
with an ambling motion, and the wind got into his great
black beard. He spoke to Hornby in a high-pitched voice
and laughed. Then he threw the ball to a tall, graceful
player just behind him and cried, 'Catch her, Bunny.'
Following Grace and Hornby were Lucas, C. T. Studd, J.
M. Read, the Hon. A. Lyttelton, Ulyett, Barlow, W. Barnes,
A. G. Steel and Peate. The crowd quietened, awaiting the
advent of Australia's first two batsmen, and I again heard
the parson's voice. ' ... The English total was distress-
ingly poor. Rarely have I seen poorer batting from an All
England Eleven. The fact is, sir, that for some little time
now English cricket has been deteriorating. Our batsmen don't hit the ball as hard as they used to do, and even
our bowling ...' Another cheer drowned his discourse.
'Bannerman and Massie,' said my companion. 'I should
imagine Bannerman's the youngest man in the match.'

The parson was prompt with his correction. 'I believe
S. P. Jones, who was twenty-one on the first of the
month, is the junior member of the two teams. Studd is,

I fancy, eleven months older than Jones. Bannerman is twenty-three at least, and Giffen is six days younger than Bannerman.'

My companion was silenced, but I ventured a question. 'How old is Spofforth?'

Pat came the answer, 'Twenty-seven on the ninth of next month.'

The crowd, including even the parson, went as quiet as a mouse as Barlow began the English bowling to Bannerman. Lyttelton, behind the wicket, crouched low. It was exactly a quarter past twelve. The next half-hour was a tumultuous prelude to the day. Bannerman was all vigilance, while Massie played one of the great innings of Test cricket. He hurled his bat at every ball the slightest loose, and his hits crashed ponderously to the boundary. He was the living image of defiance as he faced the Englishmen, glaring round the field his challenge. At one huge drive from Barlow's bowling my companion murmured, 'I've never seen a bigger hit than that at the Oval.'

But the parson overheard him. 'When the Australians were here in '78,' he said, 'W. H. Game, playing for Surrey, hit a ball from Spofforth to square-leg right out of the ground.' Still, he admitted that this Massie fellow hit them quite hard enough. In half an hour England's advantage of 38 was gone. Hornby called up bowler after bowler, Studd for Barlow, Barnes for Studd. Steel tried his hand at 56 – the sixth bowler in less than three-quarters of an hour. When Australia's score was 47 Massie lifted a ball to long-on.

'Lucas is there,' said the parson; 'he'll get it all r—— Good Lord!' For Lucas dropped the ball and blushed red as the crowd groaned out of its soul.

'Sixty-six for none,' murmured the man at my side; 'they're 28 on with all their wickets intact. If Massie prevails – ah, bravo, sir, well bowled, well bowled!' A ball from Steel had tempted Massie, and just as he jumped out it broke back and wrecked the wicket. Massie walked to the pavilion, roared home by an admiring but much relieved crowd. His innings was worth 55 to Australia, made out of 66 in less than an hour.

Bonner came next, and the English out-fields dropped deep and had apprehensive thoughts. Would not Massie's example make this bearded giant a very Jehu? But Hornby has an inspiration. He asks Ulyett to bowl instead of Steel. And Ulyett moves to the wicket like a man ploughing against a breaker, puts the last ounce of his Yorkshire strength into a thunderbolt of a ball that sends Bonner's middle stump flying. The crowd is only just getting back the breath lost in approval of this feat when Bannerman is caught by Studd at extra mid-off. Bannerman has batted 70 minutes for 13. 'Quick work for him!' says the parson. And with the broad bar of Bannerman out of the way the English bowlers begin to see daylight. Peate's slow left-hand deliveries spin beautifully, as though controlled by a string. The Australians now, save Murdoch, are just guessing. The fourth wicket falls at 75, the fifth at 79. Australia are all out 122. 'Only 85 to win,' says the parson. 'It's our game after all, though Lucas did his best to lose it.'

It was a true autumn afternoon going to its fall in grey light when WG and Hornby went to the wicket to face Spofforth and Garratt. The crowd filled the ground, but so silent was it as Grace took his guard that one could hear the *tink-tink* of a hansom cab coming closer and closer along the Vauxhall Road. Spofforth's first over was fast — he let the ball go with a quick leap, dropping his arm at the moment of release. Blackham 'stood back' when Grace was batting, but crept up for Hornby. 'Beautiful wicket-keeping', murmured my companion.

'Pinder was not less gifted,' said the parson. And he added, 'I have not seen Spofforth bowl as fast as this for some time. He has latterly cultivated medium-pace variations.' Both Hornby and Grace began confidently, and at once the tension lifted. Hornby made a lovely cut from Spofforth and a dainty leg stroke for a couple.

Spofforth uprooted Hornby's off stump with England's score 15, and with his next ball clean bowled Barlow. The crowd gave out a suspicion of a shiver, but the advent of bluff George Ulyett was reassuring, especially as Grace welcomed him with a fine leg hit from Garratt for three and a beautiful on drive to the boundary from Spofforth. 'Thirty up,' said my companion; 'only 55 to get.' England was still 30 for two when Spofforth crossed over to the pavilion end. Now I was behind his arm; I could see his superb break-back. And he bowled mainly medium pace this time. With each off-break I could see his right hand, at the end of the swing over, finish near the left side, 'cutting' under the ball. Sometimes his arm went straight over and continued straight down in the follow-through – and then the batsman had to tackle fierce top spin. There was the sense of the inimical in his aspect now. He seemed taller than he was a half-hour ago, the right arm of him more sinuous. There was no excitement in him; he was, the parson said, cold-blooded. Still Ulyett faced him bravely while Grace, at the other end, time after time moved from his crease with a solid left leg and pushed the ball away usefully.

'Fifty up,' said my companion, 'for two wickets. It's all over – we want only thirty-four now,' And at 51 Spofforth bowled a very fast one to Ulyett, who barely snicked it. It served, though; Blackman snapped the catch, and his 'H'zat!' was hoarse and aggressive. Lucas came in, and with two runs more WG was caught at mid-off.

'What a stroke!' said the parson. 'I'm afraid he's not the Grace he was.'

Four for 53, and Lyttelton and Lucas in. Lyttelton hits out big-heartedly, but the field is like a net tightly drawn. It is suddenly understood by every man of us that the game is in the balance.

'The wicket must be bad,' says somebody.

Lucas stonewalls, with a bat as straight as a die. Spofforth bowls a maiden; Boyle bowls a maiden; Spofforth bowls another maiden. The air is growing thick.

'Get runs or get out, for the Lord's sake,' says somebody.

The field creeps closer and closer to the wicket. Spofforth and Boyle are like uncanny automatons, bowling, bowling, bowling . . . Six successive maidens.

'This,' says the parson, 'this is intolerable.'

One's heart is aching for an honest boundary hit . . . And the human bowling machines send down six more successive maidens. Think of it: twelve successive maidens, and the game in that state, the crowd in that purgatory.

'When Grace was a boy of eighteen I saw him make 50 on this very ground and he played every ball he got.' It was the parson again, but he sounded a little strained, a little unhappy.

At the end of the twelfth successive maiden, a hit was purposely misfielded that Spofforth might have a 'go' at Lyttelton. The batsmen fell into the snare. Four more maidens, and spinning is Lyttelton's wicket.

'Anyhow, that's over and done with!' thankfully breathes the crowd. Better all be dead than dying! England five for 66 – 19 needed. Steel comes next and Lucas hits a boundary. Roars the crowd 'Bravo!' then catches breath. Steel caught and bowled Spofforth none – Maurice Read clean bowled second ball. England 7 for 70.

'Incredible!' say 20,000 people in dismal unison.

Barnes, the next man, hits a two. Thirteen to win. Heaven bless us, Blackman has blundered! He allows three byes. Run Barnes, run Lucas! Spofforth is inscrutable as the crowd makes its noises. His next ball is too fast for eyes at the boundary's edge to see. Lucas comes down on it, though – hard, determined. And the ball rolls ever so gently on to the wicket and disturbs the bail. Poor Lucas bows his head and departs, and blasphemy is riot throughout the crowd and is communicated by stages to the outer darkness of Kennington Road.

The stars are set against England – our cricketers are for the first time on English soil face to face with a victorious Australian XI. With ten to struggle for, Blackman catches Barnes off his glove, and the last man is here – poor Peate, who is the best slow bowler in England and not a bit more of a cricketer than that, and what good are his mysteries of spin now! Studd is there yet, though; only ten runs and it is our game. Perhaps *he* – Peate has hit a two. It was audacious, but maybe the ball was a safe one to tackle. A bad ball's a bad ball at any time. Peate has nerve (so we are telling ourselves, desperately): he's the right man: he'll play the steady game to good stuff and leave the job to Studd . . . The stark truth is that Peate hit out wildly yet again at a slow from Boyle, missed it, and was bowled. There was a hollow laugh somewhere as the wicket went back, but whether it came from this world or the next I couldn't say. Studd did not get a ball. 'Why, man, did you try to hit: why couldn't you just stop them?' they asked Peate.

'Well,' he replied, 'I couldn't trust Maister Studd!'

As Peate's wicket was broken, ten thousand people rushed the rails and hid the green field. Spofforth was carried shoulder-high to the pavilion, and there the mob praised a famous man. I, too, wanted get up and shout, but somehow I was rooted to my seat. I was probably the only man in that multitude on the pavilion not standing up, and as I sat there I had a strange sense of making a lonely hole in a solid black mass.

The parson was standing on the seat beside me. His boots were not more than two feet from my eyes and I could see the fine ribbed work on the upper edge of the soles. The cheering came downwards to me, sounding remote. I lost grip on events. It seemed that I sat there till the ground was almost deserted, till over the field came a faint mist, and with it the vague melancholy of twilight in a great city. Time to go home, I thought . . . a great match . . . great days . . . great men . . . all gone . . . far away . . . departed glory . . .

A hand of someone touched my shoulder and I heard him say: 'The Orsetralians are on the way, and they'll be in the nets at four o-clock. Nice in the sun, isn't it?'

On a Fresh Cricket Season

The beginning of cricket was fixed by Lord's for round about the first of May, and ostensibly it began then, and was duly reported in the newspapers. But here and there a cricketer of spirit was made to understand that the season was upon him before this; it came, for him, a day sooner at least than the rest of us were aware; the very instant, in fact, that a spring light woke him one morning and stirred in his mind a solitary thought: 'Today we leave for the South; today we set out on the summer's first tour.'

Nothing can go wrong with him on this blessed morning. He packs his bag blissfully, beholds the faded labels on it, eloquent of many a golden Odyssey. Lovely sequence of names – Canterbury, Taunton, Worcester, Horsham, Tonbridge! It was at Horsham, our happy cricketer tells himself, he saw the season die last August. How far away did May seem on that afternoon when the sun burned out and he packed the bag for the last time and said 'Goodbye' to his companions! Did he not wish then with all his heart for Maytime back again? Did he not then ask himself why, when the season's beginning was with him, he had not shouted for joy the day long? Well, a spring morning is here for his delight again. Let him hang on to every minute of it, revel in a delighted sense of the time of the year, tell himself over and over: 'I am getting the best out of the day as it passes; I am missing nothing!'

Observe, happy man, from your bedroom window, at this moment as you prepare yourself for a journey to the South — observe the passers-by along the road opposite. They are going to work, going to the city, there to live stuffily in one dingy spot, while you — while you are going away for the beginning of cricket. Tonight these poor souls will pass by your house again, back from the city, but you will not be there to see them return. By then you will be at the other end of England; perhaps you will have just been taken by the hotel porter to your room, just have unpacked, washed, and gone out into the delicious streets, to ravish yourself in them with the feeling of the miles you have covered that day, and also with the feeling of romantically settling down now in a new place.

Does it matter that as the tour begins our cricketer finds a train crowded as it leaves London Road Station behind, with its mile's view of slate roofs on every hand? Not a bit of it. The other people in the compartment are plainly the veriest birds of passage; prosaic shortness of distance is to be their portion. They must depart at Stockport, or at the most at Crewe. When Market Street and Deansgate are at their crisis of unloveliness and congestion, our happy cricketer is moving through green fields; he is getting intimate glimpses into country life, as from the spacious rolling view outside the carriage window his eye detaches a thatched cottage with a postman knocking at the door, or a village street lazy in noon warmth – it is underneath him now, for the train rattles thunderously over a bridge. And now it is gone!

At Wellington, or in some such place deep in the garden of our land, the journey is broken; there is a change here. The Manchester train goes out, leaving you exquisitely aware that you are now quite out of touch with Manchester. Your connection arrives – a train that obviously has never been in Manchester. The people on it have just as obviously never been in Manchester. Here, unmistakably, you are in a fresh hemisphere, entering on the journey's last lap through a drowsy landscape. And how peaceful the closing hour of a day's railway travel is! The mild agitations of the morning – felt even by a happy cricketer have spent themselves. The senses are tired at last of responding to new scenes, new sounds, new odours. Through too much unfolding of strange life about him our pilgrim feels an agreeable tedium; he drops into a reverie ... After Oxford, Cambridge, and then Leicester – always lots of fun at Leicester. Must look out for Astill's swinger, though. Yorkshire after that; suppose they'll give us the usual hot stuff. Where do we play Kent this year? Good Lord, at

Gravesend! Why not on the Angel Ground at Tonbridge – glorious place! Wonder if my off-drive will be better this year. Must get my foot to it more. That's a nice piece of wood Smith picked for me; must get it going tomorrow at Oxford. Might easily pick up runs for nothing at Oxford; always a few green bowlers there this time of the year. A good start's everything . . .

On the carriage seat he notices a newspaper, and there is a paragraph in it giving the County XI for its first match. He sees his name and is thrilled. After the winter's obscurity he is to become an item in the public news once more. In a day or two from now men in Newcastle and Woking, men he has never seen or heard of, telegraphists, sub editors, and compositors by livelihood, will be bandying his name about. 'Blank drove Benskin and completed his fifty in sixty-five minutes.' This will be read on the Manchester Exchange, in the Reform Club even, in Back George Street among the grey cloths, in Gorton, and in Westhoughton.

Will he run into form quickly? But he has no use for misgivings in this hour of May content. He is master of his fate, captain of his break-back. He sees, in his splendid vision, a hundred moments that the summer holds for him – the yellow stumps standing upright as he reaches the crease at the fall of the first wicket, with the white line of the popping crease just broken in the middle where Smith took his guard; the fieldsmen moving back to position as he gets his bat ready; the trees away in the distance behind the bowler. He sees the bowler coming towards him, face set; he feels

63

his bat circling in the air, feels the ecstasy that comes with a hit clean in the blade's middle; he sees a fieldsman on the off-side boundary picking up the ball after it has been thrown back into the field from the crowd. He sees Lord's again, basks in the sense of walking to it on a June morning down the St John's Wood Road; he sees himself 'going on at the Nursery End', the while the score-board announces 'Bowler 7' and the pavilion bloods look at their cards and pronounce his name. He sees all the lovely cricket fields in England beckoning to him; he sees the sun mellowing on an afternoon somewhere in brown Sussex as cool drink is brought and bowlers slake their thirsts, while away on the field's edge a man in white lies prone on the grass even as he, our happy cricketer, stands erect at the wicket, 86 not out. And, best vision of all, he sees himself 'not out' even to the close of play, privileged to remove his pads, to change from his warm flannels, to leave the ground, to go here, there, and everywhere that evening, to go to bed, to get up in the morning; privileged to pass through all these spaces between one day's play and another and to remain not out all the time! Moments of vision indeed. Tomorrow and tomorrow – days in the sun, luscious grass to walk on, wind running over the body. Happy man, this is the time of the year for you; August will never seem so far away again.

The train's whistle blows; pace slackens. Here you are, and the others, cricketers all, with the season well and beautifully launched. No runs yet, maybe, and no wickets down; but a paradisal day already lived through.

The Cricketer as an Artist

We are supposed to be well on the way towards decadence in an art as soon as we allow the parts to fascinate us rather more than the whole – when, for instance, a Debussy so falls in love with the attractiveness of his whole-tone scale harmonies that he neglects the main job of music, which is the expression of some sort of emotion. But decadent or no, it is only human to find great joy in a new technical dodge for its own sake. A man may decide to buy a cycle, meaning really to save money in railway fares from and to the city; none the less, the day the machine arrives he will take the thing out and ride it to nowhere in particular, simply exulting in a new toy. Probably he will also take it to pieces and lose a few important screws and things – out of what is at the bottom the artist's preoccupation with the way of doing things simply for the fascination of that way.

This love of technique for technique's sake is a charac-teristic in English cricket today – perhaps more than it has ever been before. The parts of cricket – bowling, batting, and fielding – are now reaching an almost over-developed stage. In the beginning, we can imagine, 22 men met on a field, took sides, and had no other interest in cricket than to win the match. No matter how 'old Lumpy' bowled 'Nutty' out – grub or full toss – the great point was that he was out. And the lucky snick past slip looked just as well on the score sheet as the neatest of cuts. In its earliest period, the parts of cricket were too crudely organised to invite specialism and all those distractions which specialism can easily engender to take a cricketer's attention from the job in hand – that of beating the other men. Played on a village green, rudely if lovingly, one could say of cricket, borrowing from Kipling, that 'the game was more than the player of the game.' Nothing but the lust for conquest and contest here – no wiredrawn appreciation of the fine shades; simply the wigs on the green and our team against the world.

There is a different viewpoint from this among crick-eters now, and, indeed, among watchers of cricket. Who cares about the tussle for championship points if a Ranji be glancing to leg? Even the man who wants Surrey to get beaten cannot find it in his heart to complain if Hobbs scores a hundred. And what modern bowler that has felt the joy which comes of breaking a ball from the off with a leg-break action can resist the temptation of bowling his googly in season and out – aye, even if he suspects that a good straight length ball would get his man out quicker?

A summer or two ago the writer was coaching little boys at a public school. They chafed at having to pass through a course of conventional bowling. 'We'd rather get wickets with breaks and swerves than the straight stuff that the old 'uns used to bowl' — that was their view of the matter at the bottom. And only the other day, a great batsman in one of our counties, when he was bowled trying to hook an off ball, explained his failure in these words: 'Well, you simply can't go on hitting off-balls past mid-off. Any fool is able to do that. One gets tired of doing things in the easiest way.' The divine discontent of the artist, this, surely. Who that has a soul at all, be he bricklayer or maker of sonnets, is happy just moving along the lines of least resistance? Had Ranjitsinhji been content with fat scores made in the fashionable way, he could easily have gone on hitting balls from the middle stump straight to long-on. But he was ever an artist, 'tired of doing things in the easiest way', ever seeking to widen the scope of his craft, experimenting, creating obstacles for the sheer fun of overcoming them.

Was ever cricket so well off in the so-called classical days for artists, especially artist-bowlers, as the game has been these last few years, since the advent of B. J. T. Bosanquet and his disciples? Surely a man had to have an axe of partisanship to grind before he could rave for aesthetic reasons about the bowling of the Attewell school. A good length outside the off stump all day — why, one of those new-fangled bowling machines would have been as interesting to watch. It was all right, of course, if you were watching the

67

game for no other reason than to shout Nottinghamshire home, for undoubtedly Attewell did get his bags of wickets. But the man who goes to cricket solely to witness a contest is mistaking his game. Football can work off more combative energy in ten minutes than cricket in a summer.

The summer game has, of course, its tight finishes – moments in which it is the team and not the individual that matters, moments in which one will cheer a full toss that gets a wicket and groan at the bowler whose fine off-break gets clouted for six. But these seasons of crisis come rarely in cricket. Normally the game is a spectacle as much as a contest. And because of that we must have our artist cricketers – men who can get us interested in themselves, who can get interested in themselves, even though no finish of the game is in sight, and all is moving to the drawn match which bores the uninitiated onlooker. With Attewell bowling like an automaton and Scotton always taking the line of least resistance, the game needed to be won and lost. There was little, surely, in these cricketers but match-winning qualities. And, significantly enough, with the coming in recent summers of the great individualists like Fry, Ranji, Trumper, Bosanquet, the ancient lament about incompleted games has been heard less and less.* Nobody worries about the draw – the uncompleted match which satisfies no lust for conquest – if an artist-batsman happens to be on view. Not long ago the most attractive

---

* Written in 1920.

side in the country was Sussex, with, of course, Ranji in the eleven. Yet they drew all, or nearly all, their matches.

Our grandfathers had, of course, their artist-batsmen in no small numbers, and perhaps it is in bowling that modern cricket is infinitely more interesting* than cricket of yesterday to the onlooker who does not happen to be a partisan, but watches simply out of a love of the fine shades. Certain, anyhow, that our grandfathers never knew the googly. When county groundsmen a few years ago started to make their pitches as perfect for batsmen as they knew how – mainly with an eye to a three days' gate – they probably broke the hearts of scores of average bowlers, who found that length and spin were not much use on those 'shirt-front wickets'. But the artist-bowler found only another occasion for joy in this new obstacle, and set himself to get over it. Then the googly came, the whole point of which is to deceive the batsman before the ball has pitched. What matter the state of the ground if you can beat your man in the air? And the perfect modern wicket saw also the development of the swerve – another device calculated to enable a bowler to snap his finger at the groundsman and his marl.

Thus did bowling take on finer and finer points. Today people actually go to a match to watch Parkin bowl – it is not only the batsman that is in the picture now! Mind you,

---

* 'Interesting,' I say – from the spectators' point of view; I do not mean that bowling now is better technically.

they go not merely to watch Parkin bowl somebody out. Folk doubtless went to look at Alfred Shaw get wickets. It was the wickets going down that they liked; not bowling for its own sake. A few summers ago scores of cricketers flocked to Lord's keen on Parkin's bowling and found it interesting whether or no he was getting wickets.

Specialism always makes the parts more and more interesting, and we have arrived at the time when cricket is in the hands of specialists. There is even a danger that the whole will suffer. You can get so much in love with the art of spinning the ball 'the wrong way' that you begin to forget that without a good length a bowler is no match-winner. And as a long-hop is not even pretty to watch, you might even cease to be worth looking at. It is well, then, that in cricket, too, nature in the long run distributes equally her Platonists and her Aristoteleans – the men who walk by faith and the men who walk by reason. We have yet such sturdy upholders of first principles as William Quaife and J. W. Hearne. But even Hearne bowls googlies. There is no getting away from it – it is the heyday of the cricketer artist, the man who simply will not do the job in the old fashioned and easiest way.

Cricket Fields and Cricketers

There is surely some interaction between a cricket team and the ground it mainly lives on – does not the play of the side assume tone and colour from the scene? Yorkshire cricket has the aspect of Bramall Lane and Leeds – dour, and telling of stern competitive life with smoke and real industry about. Can you imagine the shrewd Lancashire game quite at home under a June sky at the Saffrons? Does not there come through the cricket of Sussex the brown and sunny flavour of Eastbourne and Hove when the time of day is noon and the earth seems humming with heat? The plain homeliness of the Midlands is expressed by Leicestershire cricket: it has no airs and graces, no excessive refinements. See an innings by Cole, of Leicestershire, and you ought not to be long guessing from the smack of rotund nature about it that he has passed the main portion of his days in the sun on a field with rustic benches running intimately round. No, it is

not mere fancy to say: 'Show me a cricket team in action
and I'll tell you where is its native heath.'

Take Lord's, for example. The country spirit, the cir-
cumscribed life denoted by country, is not for Lord's. For
your good cricketer the ends of the earth have come to a
resting-point at Lord's, and wherever he may be at the fall
of a summer's day his face should turn religiously towards
Lord's. Lord's is the Cosmopolis of cricket. And which
county do you find playing the bulk of its games at Lord's?
Why, naturally enough, the team that, less than them all,
gives us the definite county flavour. Middlesex has ever
been as cosmopolitan as Lord's itself – a side gathered
from the earth's corners, West Indians, Australians, even
Yorkshiremen! A man from Huddersfield sat in the crowd
at Lord's a season or two ago, and as he watched Middlesex
beating his own county he was stirred to a protective derision – a derision which he cultivated as balm for the wound
that defeat at cricket must always bring to Yorkshiremen.
'Middlesex? he asked of the throng around him. 'Wheer's
Middlesex? Is it in Lundon?'

His barb was well directed; London obliterates the
county boundaries, and neither at Lord's nor at the Oval do
you feel the clannishness that stings you in the atmosphere
of Old Trafford or Bramall Lane. To be eloquent of authentic county demands a certain narrowness, a contentment
with those things of the earth, and that part of the earth,
which providence has placed immediately at one's doorstep. County means nature and at Lord's cultivation borne

on the winds of the world has rather expelled nature. Watch Hearne move fastidiously towards a century; watch Bruce or Crutchley batting, and you are looking on cricket played in the drawing-room of civilised men and woman. And at those times when Bosanquet bowled at Lord's there came into the game the touch of exquisite decadence that marks a true Cosmopolis. Frankly, I have never yet been able to fix Hendren into my notion of Lord's; he is quite indecently provincial in his relish of a thumping boundary.

There is, of course, in the life of a cultivated cricketer little that is sweeter than a summer morning at Lord's, a morning when the sky is a blue awning blown out with soft wind, and the trees at the Nursery End make a delicate motion. 'The Nursery End at Lord's!' The phrase sets memory astir, for have we not read in days of old in those evening papers our boyish eyes scanned that 'Richardson went on at the Nursery End,' that 'Ranjitsinhji glanced Noble to the rails at the Nursery End'? Because Max Beerbohm has never written an essay called 'Going to Lord's on a July Morning' we have proof he has never in his life walked down the St John's Wood Road with a day of cricket in sunny weather before him.

But perhaps it is not given to the man who lives only round the corner from Lord's and can visit it every day to feel its appeal as keenly as the man from the North, who not more than three or four times a year walks down the St John's Wood Road. Let the morning be quiet and mellow and there seems in the air about the St John's Wood Road, at least to one not too familiar with the place, a sense of the dead old days, causing a melancholy which no doubt one ought to be ashamed of. The mind is made by this something in the St John's Wood air to play with fancies of Victorian greatness hanging about the spot; of a gleaming hansom cab at the entrance and a black-bearded man, looking mountainous in everyday clothes, getting out while folk standing round murmur 'WG!'; of simple-faced men in wide, uncreased trousers proceeding along the pavement – the names of them, likely enough, Lockwood, Lohmann, Richardson – all keen to 'get at the old 'un.'

No lover of cricket as he wanders about Lord's can very well keep the thought of Grace from his mind, for though Grace was a Gloucestershire man surely he larded the green earth at Lord's till the very spirit of him may be said to have gone into the grass. You see, just as Lord's is too large in spirit to stand for any one county or for any one space of time in cricket's history, so did the amplitude of Grace transcend Gloucestershire and his little day. At Lord's, with a June morning spending its warmth, one feels a kind of resentment that there should ever have been a bourne put by nature on WG's capacity to endure and play the game till he was utterly tired of it. Is not Lord's here for him now just as ever it was, and a summer day here also, one so fresh that it casts clean out of the understanding the thought of years that pass away? Why could it ever happen to a cricketer that a June morning comes on which the sun begins in the old comfortable way to climb the sky, and

Lord's stands in the light, full of summer-time animation, and he no longer there to know of it?

II

Leave Lord's one day and tomorrow discover Bramall Lane and you enter another world. Frankly, the cricket field at Sheffield is a blasted heath, but, as Shakespeare knew, it is on blasted heaths that matters of grim moment come to pass. A Lancashire and Yorkshire match is not to be thought of at Lord's; here at Sheffield the scene tells a plain tale of the stiff energy of North Country life, and it provides the right setting for a battle between ancient hosts where the informing spirit is of a dour and combative blood feud. Squat chimneys outside the ground loom black, and even on a Bank Holiday the air contains a hint of furnaces and steel smelters. And to the man who likes his cricket moving dramatically on the right stage the Bramall Lane crowd is a work of art. It is a multitude which seemingly throws out a white heat and causes the game to boil over prodigiously.

Who at Sheffield on Whit Monday in 1922 will ever forget the great crowd that watched Yorkshire struggling for a first innings' advantage over Lancashire the day long? It was a crowd unashamedly partisan. No room had the red-hot ranks for the equanimity that can look on an issue and say: 'May the best side win.' This vast gathering lived the violent afternoon through to one thought, to one thought alone: 'Down with Lancashire. Trample the Red Rose in the dust.' Here we had a partisan temper which sought to persuade events in Yorkshire's way. There was surely not a man on Bramall Lane's desolate plain that afternoon who would not have held up his hands to the sky till pain scourged him had he believed that such a martyrdom would keep the hurly-burly favourable to his county. Not magnanimous, you might well say; still, there is an aspect to partisanship as brittle as this which is not entirely to be despised. If the Sheffield crowd cannot attend to the amenities at the sight of an advance by the ancient foe, if it is driven in the hour of Yorkshire's adversity to a fury and apprehension that have no use for a magnanimous admiration of the skill of the conquerors, we may wish ourselves far away from such a crowd, and thank our stars cricket does not breed many like it, but we certainly cannot deny that here is 'character', here is rich red blood and abundant spirit.

I have heard folk from the South say of cricket at Sheffield that it simply is *not* cricket. Their preference has been for the game as it is played with trees and country graciousness around. But why put a limit to cricket's appeal; why deny her infinite variety? Lancashire and Yorkshire at Bramall Lane is not less cricket than any match in an old meadow at Little Slocombe on the laziest day in June. Cricket, indeed, has many facets; it can satisfy most of the human animal's interests and emotions, and, as *we* have seen, it is sensitive to most of our moods and our habitations. It can stir one, at Sheffield, into a very man of war;

it can soothe one, at Tonbridge, to the sweetest peace. In turn, it can sound a clarion note that sets the combative spirits in the blood running agog like hey-go-mad, as Tristram Shandy would say; and in turn it can capture the summer's own music.

Lord's in Wet Weather

JUNE 1920

For want of something better to do during these last two incredibly wet days at Lord's, I have been trying to understand why that place so forcibly recalls Charles Dickens' *Bleak House*. It is not merely that the rain has turned the place into another Chesney Wold; that the view from the pavilion window as I write is alternately a lead-coloured view and a view in Indian ink; that the heavy drops fall, drip, drip, drip, upon the pavilion terrace, which might be named the Ghosts' Walk, since the shades of so great cricketers of other days make it murmurous. No, not simply these external and quite accidental effects are responsible for the mind's jumping back to Dickens' novel. Lord's is capable of reminding you of Sir Leicester Dedlock and Chesney Wold in fine weather as well as in wet, so inflexibly aristocratic is the place, so proud of the ceremonies, so insistent on blue blood.

Unless one happens to be definitely of Lord's, and a member of the mighty MCC, one is outside the pale here. You are inexorably kept at a distance. The place is a mass of signboards, teaching you your manners and position in life. Like Sir Leicester Dedlock all over, Lord's is as old as the hills, and, so it would appear, infinitely more respectable. The place, indeed, carries a general air of believing that the world might get on without hills, but would be done up without the MCC. Since Nature made the grass which grows there, Lord's would, no doubt, admit with Sir Leicester that, on the whole, Nature is a good idea, but an idea just a little low when not enclosed with a fence. There is even to this day at Lord's a kind of fence which separates amateurs from professionals. A man from the unfashionable North, carrying with him a suggestion of real industry, feels that Lord's is all the time eyeing him curiously from a safe point of vantage, and mentally putting him down as a possible Wat Tyler, or, at the most generous estimate, an Ironfounder.

It is hard to imagine there is any place in the world where class distinctions are so firmly stressed as at Lord's. During a University match this is more apparent than ever. That is why possibly no painter in the school of Frith has given us a canvas depicting Lord's on a fine summer's day during the occasion of a 'Varsity match. The picture would certainly give scope for something of the multitudinous panorama in Frith's too much abused *Derby Day*, but it would be bound to miss the broad universal appeal of the racing picture. Human nature on a large scale could hardly be got into a view of Lord's – only one aspect of it, well bred and exclusive. A race meeting, on the other hand, annihilates class distinctions.

What would happen to a man in corduroys (supposing for the sake of argument such a phenomenon possible) – what would happen to him if he smote a Viscount on the back in the throes of some enthusiasm for a leg hit?

Yet at a race meeting such events have been known to happen, to nobody's consternation. One touch of Epsom with the favourite in fourth at 6 to 4 on makes the whole world kin. Still, these fine aristocratic ways at Lord's do not really annoy. Possibly an American writer would find them objectionable. That is because he would not regard them, as they are regarded by the average outsider, who pays his couple of shillings at Lord's, as just a pretty decoration on the main structure of affairs.

Lord's will not allow the man in the street to come right into the swim, but they can't keep him right out. I saw a few working men this morning at the ground gates waiting for the rain to stop. They variously wore light and dark blue colours. How each man decided whether Oxford or Cambridge should be the vent for the expression of his inveterate partisanship I could not say. His interest in both elevens might have been merely academic. But it was not so – these same working men were rather hot with argument about the respective qualities of Bettington, Marriott, Hedges and Partridge.

Obviously the game is more than the player of the game, in Kipling's words, even at Lord's, and common human nature will creep in. The terrible rain today could not quite keep it out.

Spooner at Old Trafford

AUGUST 1920

The innings of Spooner in the Lancashire and Yorkshire match on August Bank Holiday will not quickly be forgotten. It was his return to the crowd that loves him after a long absence, and the magic of his art made everybody on the packed ground that day into a jubilant, shouting schoolboy. Such batsmanship had not been seen at Old Trafford since the Augustan days before the war. He went in first with Heap. Waddington gave him some trouble before he found the pace of the drying turf. We hung on to his every movement. If he should fail! Ah, be careful, Reggie, with that swinging off ball! For a while we sit in purgatory. And then the master drives Waddington gloriously to the on boundary, and we are in paradise. The master is now in tune with himself. Two off drives to the rails from successive balls off Rhodes — and then the sheerest poetry of cricket. 'Wrist-work! Wrist work!' is the usual comment on Spooner's cricket. And it really does seem that he makes his forcing strokes even as an artistic housemaid uses a feather duster. But no man could urge a ball in front of the wicket, with Spooner's strength, by wrist-work alone. There must be some latent body energy in the hit; the muscular mechanism works so smoothly that it deceives us. A fountain is a thing of fairy spray to the eye, but underground some violent pressure goes on. It may be in such wise with Spooner batsmanship.

The great man in cricket, as in all other arts, is an individualist, whose game is as much a part of him as his physiognomy (to echo Fenélon), his figure, his throbbing pulse – in short, as any part of his being which is subjected to the action of the will. In and through the art of batsmanship we have come know Spooner as intimately as if he had written 'Sonnets to a Dark Lady'. Walk at random on a cricket field and see Spooner make his off-drive. You have no need to be informed that Spooner is batting. The stroke can be 'attributed' with as much certainty as any canvas by Paul Véronèse. That graceful forward poise, the supple play of the wrists! Ranji himself was not more graceful than Spooner. There was, in fact, a disturbing melodramatic element in Ranji now and then. When he glanced to leg that straight ball dead on the middle stump, you gasped amazedly. And emotion is never pricked as sharply as that by sheer grace. In Spooner's batting, at his best, we see the unities observed (as the gentleman in Dickens would say): the harmony, the eternal fitness of the game, suffers no shock. For Spooner just puts bloom on the orthodox. His cricket has a classical purity in these days. But if his decorative formality makes him a Pre-Raphaelite, so to say, he is a Pre-Raphaelite of the Millais order – the Millais who painted *Autumn Leaves*. There is warm colour in his play as well as the clear natural outlines.

The Defeat at Eastbourne

AUGUST 1921

From the pains which entered the body of English cricket at Trent Bridge in May the good Lord has at long last delivered us. This afternoon, on the sunny Saffrons cricket field, the Australians' colours have been hauled down; the mighty men that authentic England elevens have found unconquerable in ten successive Test matches have been beaten, beaten by a fictitious England eleven under the leadership of our greatest cricket captain, and, moreover, beaten by a side that was routed in a first innings for 43 paltry runs. Who on Saturday could have got the faintest glimpse of such an end to the match, even in the wildest flight of fancy? All cricketers know well the infinite changefulness of the great game, but to overthrow the might of Australia from no better base than a first innings total of 43 – why, the miraculous is here, black magic, the very imps of mischief. There were the most thrilling fluctuations in the

85

day's play; now the game was safe in Armstrong's keeping, now it slipped from his grasp, now, by a desperate motion of the will, Armstrong clutched it again, and then, as, indeed, it looked his for good, out it slipped and MacLaren and his men stuck greedily to it.

At the morning's outset Bardsley and Carter played the bowling comfortably. Gibson was seemingly harmless, and from his first three overs 16 runs came. Would other English captains have taken Gibson off after so bad a beginning? MacLaren did not – and, true, he had no great amount of bowling at hand to embarrass him. But MacLaren has had faith in Gibson throughout the summer, and today the young University cricketer was to justify, as Barnes and Dean once justified, the insight of the master. With Australia's score 52 Gibson clean bowled Bardsley by a glorious ball that pitched on the off stump and hit the leg. Falcon then bowled a fast short one to Carter, who cut it powerfully. In the Test matches such a stroke from an Australian invariably went to the boundary. Today young Claude Ashton was in the slips; he saw the ball as a swallow sees a fly, darted forward, and caught it magnificently. The outlook for Australia was darkening, but soon the confidence of Macartney's and Andrew's cricket made slight sunshine for Armstrong. And with the total 73, Falcon bowled Macartney, who produced a weird stroke with a cross bat. Pellew and Andrews added just 30 for the fifth Australian wicket, which fell when Hubert Ashton brilliantly caught Pellew at slip. So to lunch with no man's appetite keen for food. Australia needed now 87, with five wickets in hand.

Half-an-hour's play after the interval, and surely the victory was Armstrong's entirely. Andrews and Ryder scored 34 runs in this short space, and, worst of all for MacLaren's prospects, they hit Falcon's bowling all over the field. The score was 140 for five when MacLaren asked Faulkner to bowl in place of Falcon. The move was made at the last moment, still at the right moment. Gibson broke the Ryder-Andrews partnership at last, but it was Faulkner, in his third over, that placed the Australians completely against the wall by upsetting Andrews' off stump with an excellent ball which whipped across the wicket from leg. Andrews was eighth out at 158, with but 43 wanted now for his side's victory. He was in such fine form that had he endured another fifteen minutes, especially against Falcon, he would most certainly have won the match.

Armstrong was the last hope of his team. Was it just MacLaren's good luck, or was it MacLaren's superb knowledge of cricketers that ordained that Faulkner should be bowling when Armstrong came to the wicket? For Armstrong never has been able to cope with Faulkner. Today he was sorely troubled by the South African's 'googly'. He used all his cunning to avoid Faulkner, but he had to face the music at last. And Faulkner pitched him a ball whizzing with spin on the leg stump. Armstrong lost it hopelessly, and the ball would have hit the off wicket but for Armstrong's obstructing pad. Faulkner shook the skies with a triumphant "How's that?' and Armstrong had to go. Macdonald and Mailey added nine more or less nondescript runs for the last wicket, which fell to Gibson, and rightly so. He bowled beautifully without a rest throughout the Australian innings. He has a ball which is a good imitation of Barnes's famous ball, the one that pitches on the leg stump and swings away to the off. He stuck to his task gallantly, and never allowed the crisis to upset him. In the very throes of the crisis Faulkner exploited his finger spin audaciously.

At the finish, Armstrong, in a speech to the jubilant crowd, said his men had been beaten by the better side. It is certain that England in the Test matches could not show the superb fielding, the skilful and intelligent bowling of this side of MacLaren's. The fielding indeed was up to Australian standards. The crowd roared for MacLaren at the close, but MacLaren was rather overcome with emotion, and through a deputy announced this was his farewell to cricket. A beautiful farewell it has been, putting the crown on his greatness. Not in his hey-day did he give us finer captaincy than he has given us in this match. It was plain this afternoon that his very presence in the field gave his men hope and courage.

Let nobody get the impression that the Australians flung this game away through a casual attitude towards it. Possibly there was just half-an-hour of negligent batsmanship when the Australians went in against a total of 43. But from the fall of Collins' wicket on Saturday, Armstrong had his men strung taut enough. And this afternoon Armstrong's face as he witnessed the breaking of Andrews' wicket – which was a certain omen of the end – had a profoundly sombre expression. Gone the old affability! Where were his quips and oddities now?

The main causes of the Australian defeat, as it seemed to the writer, were fielding just as brilliant as the Australians' own, captaincy that put every fieldsman in the proper place, and clever spin bowling. As one watched the Ashtons, fleet of foot, sure of grasp, one thought of the heavy, plodding wanderings of England's Test match outfielders. And as one saw MacLaren move his men here and there by the most deliberate yet the gentlest waves of the hand – gestures telling of a perfectly composed mind – one thought of Douglas's volubility as he sought to obtain a tactful disposition of his men. There was, indeed, a tincture of bitterness in the sweet as one watched the afternoon proceed to its superb consummation.

The bowling of Gibson and Faulkner in the Australian second innings was just of that kind Australian batsmen have never really mastered. Barnes could put even Trumper at his mercy by the ball that broke away from the bat after pitching somewhere near the leg and middle stumps. Both Gibson and Faulkner exploited this dangerous ball this afternoon and by excellent fortune they both managed also a capital length. The Australians did not again find Falcon troublesome, though he bowled not a bit below his Saturday's form. Fast and fast-medium bowling, right arm, that comes more or less straight through, is the stuff Australian batsmen thrive on. They waxed fat on Howell, Douglas, Jupp and Parkin (when he bowled fast). To these bowlers they could play forward confidently. Even the slow-medium off-break rarely troubles an Australian batsman. He commonly is good at leg-side play and can get back to the wicket and force the ball away in the spin's direction. The ball that pitches on the wicket and breaks away he has never mastered. One might add, what batsmen have? This delivery demands the most discreet use of the 'two-eyed stance', of back play supported judiciously by the pads. And though the Australians can play back cleverly enough on slow wickets, back play is not so much in the blood of them that they can play back easily on a fast wicket.

The finger spin used by Faulkner and Gibson today is to be tackled safely only by the perfect back-play technique employed, say, by Taylor, the South African, against Barnes, a year or two ago. Armstrong's struggles with Faulkner were pathetic; he merely lunged at the ball when it was in the air, lost it as it spun, then desperately changed his stance at the last minute. Bardsley played forward beautifully to the ball that bowled him, and had it come through straight he would have hit it. The ball spun several inches on pitching, and Bardsley had no pads there as a second line of defence. A lot of abuse has been hurled at the 'two-eyed stance', and rightly, since it has too often been exploited against fast bowling. But, as this afternoon's Australian batsmanship has shown, there is not much hope against a ball spinning away at a good length if one uses the old-time lunge forward.

But the impressions of this glorious match likely to last longest are of Maclaren. One will see him, white-haired and beautifully calm, standing in the slips beckoning a man to a more judicious place in the field. One will see him plucking at his trousers' knees in the old way, hitching them up before he slightly bends into the classic slip position. One will see him moving across the pitch at the over's end, taking now and then one of his bowlers by the arm and giving him a word of encouragement and advice. And if these impressions should fade in a while, surely one will never forget his walk to the pavilion at the game's end, the crowd pressing round him and cheering – MacLaren with his sweater over his shoulders, his face almost lost in the folds of it, looking down on the grass as he moves for good from the cricket field, seemingly but half aware of the praisegiving about him, seemingly thinking of other times.

Woolley: An Appreciation

You must see Woolley batting on one of Kent's cricket fields to enjoy thoroughly the charm of his delightful art. Of course Woolley can spread beauty about him wherever he goes, but at Bramall Lane – even at Old Trafford – one thinks of him as one thinks of a butterfly in a city street on a summer's day. The writer once saw Woolley the batsman set ideally, and never will he forget it. It was while an August afternoon turned to evening in Kent. The tumult and the shouting of the day were over, and now we all sat in quiet, just waiting for stumps to be drawn while Kent played out time in the calm light. Woolley made gentle movements with his bat. His body would fall a little forward as he flicked a ball to the off-side; there seemed no weight in him when he negligently trotted down the pitch.

And as the sun shone more and more aslant, the light seemed to put this batsmanship of Woolley's under a glass; we had cool and polished contours given to it, the hard outlines of reality were lost in soft shades. Woolley's batting is frequently called 'brilliant'; it is the wrong word for his art at any time. Brilliance hints at a self-conscious gesture, of some flaunting of ability. And nobody ever has seen the touch of the braggart, or even of the coxcomb, in Woolley. The condition whereby grace has its being is a perfect unawareness of the fact that it is graceful. In grace there is always a sense of modesty; the arrogance that masterfulness breeds does not go with grace, which is one of the gentler virtues.

This is not to hint that in Woolley's batsmanship there lurks a timid spirit. We all know that Woolley is one of the world's greatest match-winning batsmen. One wishes to establish nothing more than that a batsman so winsome as Woolley is not properly to be called 'brilliant'. The word's very mention fills the mind with lurid colour. In Woolley's batsmanship there is radiance, but never a light that is garish. Even when he drives in front of the wicket the softest splendour falls over the field. None of us of these times has seen a left-handed cricketer play a handsomer game than Woolley's. To describe his forward hits one is tempted to borrow Nyren's words about Silver Billy Beldham: 'One of the most beautiful sights that can be imagined, and which would have delighted an artist, was to see him make himself up to hit a ball.' Yet the phrase will not quite fit Woolley. 'Make himself up' is too strong a term: it denotes a sudden accumulation of energy to be seen by the eye – an act of violence. Woolley has not been known to look violent or to seem stung suddenly into effort. He does not, like, say, a K. L. Hutchings or a Hirst, use a bat as a rod of punishment and flog boundaries by force out of bowlers. Rather a bat is a wand in Woolley's hand: he makes enchanting passes with it.

Woolley causes batting to appear the easiest pastime in the world. A fast bowler, pounding heavily to the crease, bowling at Woolley with the loud grunts of unloosened energy, working himself to death in the hot sun in quest of Woolley's wicket – and Woolley, all restful curves, making his easy opposition! What a contrast, and what a nice irony in it! Woolley hardly ever seems to hit a ball: of him you can really say that his strokes are *strokes*. Surely he just caresses the ball with a bat of velvet surface. One day an assertion of some primitive nature left somewhere in Woolley will impel him to smite once with all his might, and then the ball will pass far beyond the fields of Kent. For the force even of his caresses is strong enough; the secret of his motive power is timing.

He gives us the lyrical in batsmanship, just as Trumper gave us the dramatic. When Trumper batted, he met the onslaught of the bowler with an onslaught of his own as vehement. There was a conflict of will and skill when Trumper and a fast bowler were face to face, and so we had the dramatic, which thrives on conflict. As we have seen, Woolley does not look to be in stern opposition against a furious attack; he meets it effortlessly. And because drama cannot be felt unless we are made to understand that conflict hot and bitter is present, we get no drama from Woolley. He just goes his own sweet ways. While other batsmen turn the wicket into a battleground, the bowlers into an enemy to be plundered for runs, Woolley makes a soothing music that lures everybody after him, bowlers and all, as he moves along his happy track. He does not bat for his runs; he bats a serene course to them. So easeful and natural does a long innings strike you, when Woolley passes through one, that you well might think of some act blessedly predestinate.

And it is likewise when Woolley fails; you are not outraged, you are not made to think that here ambition and skill have been frustrated. In Woolley's failures there is no jar that hurts you – they are as becoming as his conquests. Grace, one has already said, is modest, and has the air of fragility always. Rude human nature, such as Hirst showed us in his pulls to the on boundary, never peeps out of Woolley. His batsmanship has been through a purifying fire; refinement one day came to Woolley

'And whipped the offending Adam out of him . . .'

The point for technical men about Woolley's batting is important; he achieves his style mainly by back play – and have we not been told time after time by the dons of the game that if a batsman would own a beautiful style he must cultivate the forward method? In Woolley you find working to perfection the modern principle: 'Play back if you cannot

95

drive.' How many times in a long innings does Woolley exploit the forward lunge, made from a rigid back foot? The writer does not recollect having seen Woolley use this stroke. Woolley has a great height and consequently a wide swing for all his hits – so wide that in the curve of one full swing are included the three points at which a half-volley, a good-length ball, and a rather short one may be struck. Woolley, then, does not need to move his feet extensively; he has only to 'time' accurately his swing down as the three different lengths come to him – which three lengths, of course, are the common lengths of bowling. Granted the slightest readjustment of the feet, Woolley's swing will serve in itself for a strong hit from any of these lengths.

His height, then, makes grace hard to miss by one so naturally willowy (let us overlook the faint suggestion of gawkiness in him); the small batsman – a Bobby Abel – is compelled to nip backwards and forwards on his feet, as the varying lengths come along, and though his animation is often thrilling, it must of necessity let the graceful go hang. Woolley has all the strokes; his leg glances, with his tall body half turning and drooping ever so slightly over to the on-side, are not magical like Ranji's were, but they are, in a quieter way, as precious. But discussion of Woolley in terms of technique is abominable. Who would talk of the *Mona Lisa* in the painter's jargon? And speaking of the *Mona Lisa*, is there not always about Woolley's dark face an inscrutable hint of a smile held back, like that we get from the lady sitting among the rocks?

Woolley's bowling was fashioned by the Tonbridge nursery, and Blythe served as the model. But the way of Nature after she has turned out a masterpiece is to break the mould. She does not let her best things get common: a solitary Blythe was enough for her; she made him once and for all. Woolley as a bowler is excellent on doubtful wickets, but he is plainly a bowler who is happier with a bat in his hands. He first trod a county cricket field at Old Trafford in Whit Week, 1906. And some of us that were in the crowd thought we had seen the beginning and the end of this tall, pale boy's experience in big cricket. It was the match in which J. T. Tyldesley cut and drove the Kent bowling for 295 not out. On the first day Woolley missed two catches; his bowling analysis when 'JTT' had finished with it was 1 wicket for 103; and in Kent's first innings Cuttell bowled him first ball. On the last day, though, he hit 64, and discerning men on the ground said the innings heralded a new glory coming into Kent cricket.

Woolley is the most stylish professional batsman in the country; his style carries the Tonbridge stamp. Kent have rarely, in fact, had an uncultivated professional batsman. They consider in Kent that a boy needs to be taught to use his blade in the way that a boy with music in him is taught in other places to use a violin; batsmanship at Tonbridge, in short, is regarded as an art and a science and therefore a matter for culture.

Cricket at Dover

KENT V LANCASHIRE, 1, 2 AND 3 JULY 1926

Wednesday

The distance from Lord's to the Dover cricket field is farther than the crow flies or even than the train travels. Here we find a different habitation than cosmopolitan Lord's: here is Kent and real England. The Dover field is tucked away in hills along which Lear must have wandered on his way to the cliffs. There are green lawns and terraces rising high behind the little pavilion, and you can sit here and look down on the play and see the cricketers all tiny and compact. In such a green and pleasant place as this, with June sunlight everywhere, slow cricket by Lancashire has not seemed quite so wearisome as usually it does. The absence of animated play has gone well in tune with the day's midsummer ease and generous warmth. We have been free to watch the game idly and give ourselves up with lazy delight to the June charm and flavours of a field all gay with tents and waving colours; and we have been free to observe the delicious changes in the passing hour – the full light of noon, the soft, silent fall to mellow.

The gentle tap-tap-tapping of the Lancashire bats has made the quiet music proper to this gracious Kentish place and occasion. On a perfect wicket Lancashire made a poor prelude to the innings. Hallows was twenty-five minutes getting his first run, and with the total 24 he sent a puny stroke to short leg and was caught at leisure. Ernest Tyldesley and Makepeace then played the steady Kent attack with a like steadiness. At lunch, after ninety minutes' action, Lancashire's score was 60 for one, and on the whole Makepeace had revealed himself our quickest maker of runs.

Between lunch and tea, two hours and a quarter, Lancashire added 135 for the loss of the wickets of Makepeace and Tyldesley. These batsmen built a part-nership worth 100 in 105 minutes. They showed us good cricket enough, but it was always kind to the bowling. Tyldesley was missed in the slips at 15, and got himself out by a half-hit to mid-on. I wish his batting were a little more masculine this year. Tyldesley and Makepeace persisted for the same period – two hours and 35 minutes. After Watson had let us see half a dozen strokes I chanced with myself a half-crown wager that he would make 50 at least. Watson's cricket, though slow, had always a more certain touch than anything he has done of late. One or two of his cover drives possessed a decisive strength I have not seen him use since last year he played an innings of a century at Lord's and delighted the heart of poor Sydney Pardon, who, alas! did not live to see his dreadful Australians considerably humbled yesterday on the cricket field he loved so dearly. Watson reached 50 in one hour and three-quarters, which apparently is the standard rate of movement nowadays in the making of a cricketer's innings. Watson seemed to give a chance to the slips at 28. Halliday struck too late at a fast medium length, after giving some hint of an ability to get his bat well over the ball. Lancashire's score arrived at 200 in ten minutes short of four hours – Poppy and Mandragora of cricket.

The Kent attack rarely fell for accuracy. Collins, Ashdown and Wright each exploit the fast to medium length which drops cannily just on the short side. Only batsmen with late, wristy strokes are able to get rapid runs against this style of attack, and, truth to say, Lancashire is not rich in wristy cricketers. Freeman's spin came from the ground with little venom, but his pitch and direction were reliable throughout all his labours. His flight has scarcely the clever variations of Mailey's bowling. To the lovely afternoon's close the Lancashire batting remained true to type.

Lancashire 307 for 8 (F. Watson 78, H. Makepeace 71, E. Tyldesley 69).

Thursday

We have had another lovely day and plenty of fascinating cricket. The Kent innings began at noon under a sky that was like a dome of glass all stained blue. On such a morning as this, a batsman is certain to see visions and dream dreams as he comes to the ground eager for the game. And Hardinge and Ashdown started to make runs with easy, confident strokes. In half an hour the Kent score reached 39, and the Lancashire men must quickly have resigned themselves to hours of sweaty toil in the warmth of a sun whose rays of light hit the hard earth like blows from a golden rod. But the chances of cricket hang on a hair's breadth. McDonald's first 41 balls were hit for 29 runs, and he did not seem to be in a conquering mood. Another six balls without a wicket would, I think, have ended with McDonald going out of action and taking a longish rest. It was at this period of incipient crisis for Lancashire and McDonald that Ashdown was guilty of a foolish mistake. McDonald had been trying to bump them — a certain proof that he was not feeling at his best. Ashdown tried to hit one of these bumpers to leg, and instead of standing up straight and to the side of the ball and exploiting the authentic hook stroke, he scooped with a blind bat, ducked his head, and sent a skier to the leg side, where Duckworth held a clever running catch.

This unlooked-for success obviously caused McDonald to lift up his heart. His pace became faster immediately, and yet again was he encouraged by thoughtless batsmanship.

Hardinge once or twice held out an indiscreet bat to quick lengths on the off side and was lucky not to touch them. The warnings taught him no lesson: again he put forth a highly experimental bat to one of McDonald's fast rising balls, and Duckworth caught him behind the wicket, crowing in glee like a cock as he did so. McDonald realised, in the style of a good opportunist, that he was in fortune's good books: he worked up a lot of his true speed, pitched a length on or near the off wicket. Seymour made a sheer reflex action and sent a slip-catch to Richard Tyldesley. Chapman also flicked a speculative bat, though this time the ball was much too close to the wicket to be left alone. Chapman was Duckworth's third victim in ten minutes.

The match in this brief space of time wheeled round dizzily in Lancashire's way. McDonald got the wickets of Ashdown, Seymour, Hardinge, and Chapman in nine balls for three runs. This merciless exposure of Kent's want of acquaintance with authentic fast bowling reduced the crowd to a silence which was broken – at least where I was sitting – only by the emphatic statement of an old gentleman to the effect that modem cricketers cannot cut, and, moreover, that Jack Mason and Burnup would have cracked this bowling of McDonald far and wide – a strong opinion indeed, announced with much ferocity of tone and addressed to nobody in particular.

The Kent batsmen, no doubt, played McDonald feebly. Several of them merely thrust out their bats to the line of the ball, using arm strength only, and not getting the body over and into a resolute stroke. Woolley threatened for twenty minutes to stem the onrush of McDonald. He drove him to the off boundary with rare power and beauty, and then sent a cut past point like the flash of valiant steel. I settled myself down to enjoy a dramatic sight – Woolley and McDonald as antagonists: Woolley standing erect at the wicket waiting with his curving bat as McDonald ran his sinuous run along the grass: Woolley flashing his lightning and McDonald hurling his thunderbolts. This spectacle of grandeur did not, as they say, materialise outside of the mind's eye: Watson suddenly and comprehensively bowled Woolley even before some of us were aware he had begun to take part in the Lancashire attack. The ball scattered Woolley's leg wicket out of the earth: it pitched between the off and middle stumps and went with the bowler's arm. The Australians would gladly pay Watson £100 for the sole rights to that excellent delivery.

The downfall of Woolley, fifth out at 74, knocked the decisive nail in the coffin of Kent's first innings. It is true that Hubble batted brightly for a while and also Freeman, but the lustre of their cricket was only like that of a sort of brass plate on the aforementioned coffin. The innings closed at three o'clock for a total which was an insult to the splendid turf. Duckworth was in reliable form: he made five catches and also accomplished a very easy case of stumping. His high-pitched shout of 'How's that' was constantly in the summer air: shall we call him chanticleer of wicket-keepers?

The other day Mr Warner wrote that English batting has improved vastly since Armstrong beat us in this country. As I watched McDonald get his wickets today I was convinced that Collins would win the Test matches almost as comfortably as Armstrong did if he commanded the McDonald and Gregory of 1921. English batting has not improved since then against really fast bowling – a melancholy truth which McDonald will demonstrate for us on any day that finds him in his strongest form.

Green rightly did not compel Kent to follow on: McDonald was tired and the wicket perfect. Makepeace and Tyldesley forced the runs excellently after Hallows had got out: 50 was reached in little more than half an hour. Makepeace scored 37 in 50 minutes – furious driving for him. Ernest Tyldesley was brilliant: not for many a long day has his cricket been so powerful, so handsome, so masterful as in this innings. He played Lancashire's proper game from the outset, drove in front of the wicket with a superb poise of body, and reached 50 in 70 minutes. No English innings in the Test at Lord's the other day, save perhaps Woolley's on Tuesday, could compare with this by Tyldesley in point of beautiful and versatile strokes. Moreover, the Kent attack was on the whole as good as the Australians', at any rate until Tyldesley hammered it off its length. This is the kind of batsmanship we need for the winning of Test matches within three days.

Tyldesley arrived at his century in two hours and five minutes without a shadow of a mistake. Iddon played strong cricket, too, and this time his forcing drives were proportionately blended with strokes of sound defence. He has still much to learn of the art of picking out the right ball for a safe hit, but he is going along nicely. In Lancashire's second innings Cornwallis did not field because of an injury to his leg. Cornwallis, by the way, is a true Kent captain – keen, chivalrous, and always in love with the game, Iddon and Tyldesley scored 122 for the fourth wicket in 90 minutes. We have seen a Lancashire eleven today in which we could take a pride indeed.

Lancashire 336 and 243 for 5 (E. Tyldesley 144 not out); Kent 154 (E. A. McDonald 7 for 81).

Friday

Green closed the Lancashire innings last night, and Kent had the whole of this cool and pleasant day for the making of 424 needed to bring them a famous victory. Five hours and ten minutes of play were to be gone through. A bad beginning happened to the innings; with only a dozen scored Ashdown tried a leg hit from Sibbles, and the ball seemed to swing in from outside his legs astonishingly, and it clean bowled his leg wicket. Seymour, who is not at all a defensive batsman but needs must play the old Kentish game of chivalry, hit ten runs off three balls from Sibbles, and attempted a stroke to the on from a short bumper sent by McDonald. He skied the ball high to leg, and Halliday, running from somewhere near mid-wicket on the on-side, made an admirable running catch, taking his prize as it dipped away from him in the wind. Even with this unfortunate prelude Kent's score reached 80 in an hour – cricket is always a game for Kent, rarely a penitential labour.

Woolley and Hardinge joined partnership at five minutes to twelve, and in ninety-five minutes they lifted the total from 41 to 181 – which brought us to lunch. The cricket was never in the least rash or demonstrative; indeed, Woolley batted half an hour for eleven. The runs came by play in which defence and offence were mingled with the most accurate judgement conceivable. The good ball was treated soundly and cautiously; the indifferent ball was seen quickly by both batsmen, and hit hard by means of a splendid range of scoring strokes. On present form Hardinge is one of the best batsmen in the land. Today his cricket was beyond criticism – solid yet antagonistic. He plays as straight a bat as any English cricketer; he can cut, drive, and glance to leg with the best of them. His batsmanship always shows to us the pre-war stamp.

Hardinge made his fifty in ninety minutes: Woolley was twenty minutes quicker over the same score. Just before lunch Woolley in getting his fifty sent a hit to third man that Hallows might possibly have caught had he made ground with some alacrity. Hardinge came to his century after two hours and three-quarter's handsome activity. At twenty minutes to three Kent wanted 224 with two and a half hours still to go. A slight drizzle hereabout damped the grass, and probably added to the hardships of a failing Lancashire attack. Woolley was badly missed by Richard Tyldesley when his score was 82, and Kent's 220 – a blunder which must have caused the whole Lancashire side to shudder from head to foot. Woolley got his beautiful hundred out of a total of 239 in two hours and ten minutes; his next stroke, a great on-drive, made the Woolley-Hardinge stand worth 200 – hit in 140 minutes. At three o'clock Kent were 170 runs from victory's goal, and two hours and ten minutes remained.

Green rung the changes on his bowlers, but all of them seemed merely so much fuel to the brilliant bonfire of batsmanship which was burning for the glory of Kent cricket before our eyes. Three fieldsmen stood on the edge of the offside field for Woolley – a rare sight in these days. The Lancashire cricketers looked rather broken in wind now: there was little hurry in their feet and apparently not much hope within their breasts. Every other ball bowled, it seemed, was hit to the distant parts of the ground: it was the fieldsmen near the wicket who had least work to do.

At 294 Woolley was leg before wicket: in two hours fifty minutes he had shown us his own delectable art and helped Hardinge to make 253 for the third wicket. With no increase in Kent's position R. Tyldesley broke through Hardinge's defence and missed the wicket by an inch: his face, red as a moon of blood, wore the aspect of anguish as he saw Hardinge escape.

It was a bolt out of Kent's blue sky that finished Hardinge's great innings – a lion-hearted quick throw-in by Green from long-on hit his wicket with Hardinge out of his ground. But for this mishap I imagine Kent would have won easily. Hardinge batted ten minutes short of four hours and a half, and deserved a more fortunate end. The cricket of Hardinge and Woolley taught a lesson which at the moment is needed in our game – the ancient lesson that offence skilfully exploited is the best form of defence. Collins was bowled, fifth out, at 327.

Tea was taken at four o'clock with Kent 341 for five – 20 minutes to be wasted, 85 runs wanted by Kent, and five wickets by Lancashire. Anybody's game and a moment of palpitating crisis in which a tea interval was an absurd irrelevance. Why should there be tea intervals at all on the closing day, on which, of course, stumps are drawn at half-past five? The heady situation challenged the audacity of Chapman, who flashed his bat like a sword at McDonald's off ball: he cut and carved 49 in fifty minutes, and then, as the game was coming again well into Kent's grip, he was neatly caught at cover by Makepeace, sixth out at 361. The next ball bowled Deed: thus a sudden heave of the game's great wheel landed the laurels at Lancashire's grasp. And McDonald's next ball shattered Wright's stumps – a hat-trick for McDonald at the very moment every Lancashire cricketer must have been praying for the miracle which alone could pull our county out of the fire lit by Hardinge and Woolley.

As Hubble and Freeman took up the defence of the Kent ninth wicket the band on the edge of the grass made the mellow music of the madrigal out of *The Mikado*. The moment was too tense, perhaps, for these golden strains, yet their sweetness was in tune with the afternoon's lovely English flavour. To my dying day I shall remember gratefully these afternoons in Kent, afternoons full of the air and peaceful sunshine of imperishable England. McDonald bowled at a noble pace during this last act of a memorable game, and as he ran his silent run of sinister grace the scene was one of those that do cricket honour – the crouching slips, the dogged batsmen, and the crowd watching, hoping, and fearing, now dumb and now making exuberant noises as some lightning stroke beat the field. McDonald bowled Freeman at 390: the little man had shown himself a fighter. Two runs afterwards Hubble was stumped exactly on the stroke of five o'clock.

And so a noble match was nobly won and, what is as true, nobly lost by 33 runs. Both sides did the grand old game service on this July day. Every cricketer played hard and passed through his difficult hours. The running out of Hardinge was the afternoon's turning-point: the splendid feat of McDonald settled the issue. He bowled finely at the finish, and Richard Tyldesley bowled finely too. A match well worth remembering – the brilliance of Hardinge, Woolley, and Ernest Tyldesley, the changeful hurly-burly of Kent's Titanic second innings – and everything done in a beautiful cricket field.

Lancashire 336 and 243 for 5 dec.; Kent 154 and 392 (F. E. Woolley 137, H. T. W. Hardinge 132, McDonald 5 for 106). Lancashire won by 33 runs.

Hobbs in the Nets

Not long ago I had the good fortune to see Hobbs at practice. He used a beautiful white bat, and as he made stroke after stroke he would glance solicitously at the face of his blade as though he were reluctant to do it hurt. The noise made by his hits was music to every cricketer present – a clean, solid noise, with no overtones. One could imagine, and envy, the thrill of delight that passed through Hobbs as he made these strokes – delight running its current from the bat's end up the arms, down the spine, and all over the body. Batsmen in other nets ceased their ineffectualities as Hobbs practised; they ceased them for very shame and also because the art of Hobbs held them in thrall.

Hobbs himself was not in serious vein. He was merely improvising like the pianist who lets his fingers move irresponsibly and experimentally over the keyboard; like the artist who in a 'rough study' will indulge in bold 'chancy' sweeps of the crayon. But it is during these improvisatory moments that we sometimes get a peep that takes us deeper into the mind and character of an artist than his finished work permits. The finished work often gives you the artist 'dressed up for the occasion', so to speak. He is, of course, himself in a finished work, but plus something conditioned by his medium and his public. It is by means of his improvisations that the artist can break free from the tyranny of his medium.

A quarter of an hour of Hobbs in the nets revealed to us a Hobbs above that ruthless law which, by the grim paradox of all art, is the source of perfection and the death of it. Here was a Hobbs free to use his bat as waywardly as he chose, and every stroke he made was made to serve no ends other than the artist's. The strokes were worth nothing in runs – no Surrey axe had to be ground in the nets. They were strokes thrown away on the air, squandered by our greatest batsman in a moment that found him free to the uttermost. In a quarter of an hour only three balls passed Hobbs's bat. The practice almost guaranteed that this summer will find him as masterful as ever.

From behind the net the technique of Hobbs is, so to speak, seen under a magnifying lens. Or it is as though one were looking at a painting with one's eyes almost glued to the canvas. You can see that now more of energy, even of roughness, goes into Hobbs's cricket than is apparent when watching him from a distance. He grips his bat in the middle of the handle as he waits for the ball, but frequently when he plays back the right hand drops almost to the bottom of the handle. This denotes strong right forearm leverage in Hobbs's defensive strokes. Immediately the bowler begins his run Hobbs seems to have some instinct of what manner of ball is on the way; rarely does he move his feet to an incorrect position. His footwork is so quick that even from behind the nets it is not always possible to follow its movement in detail.

And he covers a lot of ground – forward and backward. No wonder it is almost impossible to pitch a length to Hobbs when he is at his best. His style, like the style of the master of every art, and of every fine art, seems to sum up all that has gone before in the development of his technique. Hobbs's batsmanship has enough in it of the straight bat and the forward left foot to link it up with the batsmanship of Grace and the other old masters. Yet his on-side strokes, which he makes from a full-fronted stance, are sufficiently modern. The glorious truth is that many an honourable sowing by cricketers of the past comes to a fine flower in the batsmanship of Hobbs.

Bradman, 1930

The power of genius in cricket is not to be measured by the scoreboard, and not even by the clock. A Trumper, a Spooner, will reveal art and energy in one or two personal strokes or by some all-pervading yet indefinable poise and flavour. At Leeds Bradman announced his right to mastership in a few swift moments. He made 72 runs during his first hour at the wicket, giving to us every hit of cricket except the leg glance.

But long before he had got near the end of his innings he was repeating himself; it was as though the sheer finish of technique was a prison for his spirit. He could not make a hazardous flight; he reminded me of the trapeze performer who one night decided to commit suicide by flinging himself headlong to the stage, but could not achieve the error because his skill had become infallible, a routined and mechanical habit not at the beck and call of anything so volatile as human will or impulse. When Bradman passed

200 at Leeds I felt that my interest in his play might break out anew at the sight of one miscalculated stroke. But none was to be seen. His cricket went along its manifold ways with a security which denied its own brilliance. Every fine point of batsmanship was to be admired; strokes powerful and swift and accurate and handsome; variety of craft controlled by singleness of mind and purpose. Bradman was as determined to take no risks as he was to hit boundaries from every ball the least loose – his technique is so extensive and practised that he can get runs at the rate of 50 an hour without once needing to venture romantically into the realms of the speculative or the empirical. The bowler who had to tackle Victor Trumper was able to keep his spirit more or less hopeful by some philosophy such as this: 'Victor is moving at top speed. Well, I'm bound sooner or later to send along a really good ball. Victor will flash at it in his ecstasy-and I'll have him.' The bowler toiling at Bradman cannot support himself by a like optimism. For hours he will see his ordinary balls hit for fours along the grass; then his good one will wheel from his arm, by the law of averages which causes every bowler to achieve one moment of excellence in every hour.

But is Bradman ever likely to be so blinded by the radiance of his own visions that he will throw back his head at the good ball, confuse it with the others, and lose his wicket through a royal expense of spirit? Not he; he sees the dangerous ball with eyes as suspicious as those of a Makepeace. Down over his bat goes his head; the blade becomes a broad protective shield – and probably two pads will lend a strong second line of defence. It is not a paradox to imagine some bowler saying to Bradman, with strict justice, after Bradman has punished five fours in one over and cannily stopped the sixth ball: 'For the Lord's sake, Don, do give a fellow a chance and have a hit at her!'

The genius of this remarkable boy consists in the complete summary he gives us of the technique of batsmanship. In every art or vocation there appears from time to time an incredible exponent who in himself sums up all the skill and experience that have gone before him. It is not true that Bradman has inaugurated a new era in batsmanship: he is substantially orthodox in technique. Nearly all his strokes at Leeds could very well have been used as illustrations to C. B. Fry's thoroughly scientific and pragmatic book on batsmanship. But Bradman shows us excellences which in the past we have had to seek in different players; nobody else has achieved Bradman's synthesis. It is, of course, a synthesis which owes much to the fact that Bradman stays at the wicket longer than most of the brilliant stroke players of old ever dreamed of staying.

Perhaps he is marked off from the greatest of his predecessors not so much by technique as by temperament. It is hard to believe in the possibility of a more masterful stroke player than Trumper was, or Hobbs in his heyday. But when Trumper and Hobbs were great batsmen it was customary for cricketers to try to get out when their scores went beyond, say, 150. How many times has Hobbs thrown his wicket away after reaching his century? Bradman brings to an extensive technique the modern outlook on cricket: a hundred runs is nothing to him; he conceives his innings in terms which go far beyond Trumper's or Macartney's most avaricious dreams. He has demonstrated that a batsman can hit forty-two boundaries in a day without once giving the outfielders hope of a catch; he has kindled grand bonfires of batsmanship for us. But never once has he burned his own fingers while lighting them.

When I think of an innings by Macartney I do not think entirely of cricket. My impressions of Macartney's batting are mixed up with impressions of Figaro, Rossini's Figaro, a gay trafficker with fortune, but a man of the world; hard as iron though nimble of wit; an opportunist wearing a romantic feather in his cap. And when I think of an innings by Trumper I see in imagination the unfurling of a banner. Not by Bradman is the fancy made to roam: he is, for me, a batsman living, moving, and having his being wholly in cricket. His batsmanship delights one's knowledge of the game; his every stroke is a dazzling and precious stone in the game's crown. But I do not find his cricket making me think of other and less tangible things: the stuff of his batsmanship is skill, not sensibility. In all the affairs of the human imagination there must be an enigma somewhere, some magical touch that nobody can understand and explain. You could never account for Macartney, Ranjitsinhji, Spooner, Trumper, in terms of even a marvellous technique. Bradman, as I see and react to him, is technique *in excelsis*. I could write a textbook on him with comprehensive and thoroughly enlightening diagrams. Could anybody have written a textbook saying anything that mattered about the batting of Johnny Tyldesley?

The really astonishing fact about Bradman is that a boy should play as he does – with the sophistication of an old hand and brain. Who has ever before heard of a young man, gifted with quick feet and eyes, with mercurial spirits and all the rapid and powerful strokes of cricket – who has ever heard of a young man so gifted and yet one who never indulged in an extravagant hit high into the air? Until a year or two ago Bradman had seen little or no first-class cricket.

Yet here is he today, bringing to youth's natural relish for lusty play with a cricket bat a technical polish and discretion worthy of a Tom Hayward. A mis-hit by Bradman – when he is dashing along at fifty runs an hour – surprises us even as a mis-hit by Hayward did when he was in his most academic vein. How came this Bradman to expel from him all the greenness and impetuosity of youth while retaining the strength and alacrity of youth? How did he come to acquire, without experience, all the ripeness of the orthodox – the range and adaptability of other men's accumulated years of practice in the best schools of batsmanship? The cricket of Trumper at the age of 21 could not be accounted for, but we were content to accept it in terms of spontaneous genius. Besides, there was always the rapture and insecurity of the young man in Trumper. But while we can account for Bradman's batting by reason of its science and orthodoxy, we are unable quite to accept it – it is too old for Bradman's years and slight experience. The genius who thrills us is always unique but seldom abnormal. If Bradman develops his skill still further – and at his age he ought to have whole worlds to conquer yet – he will in the end find himself considered not so much a master batsman as a phenomenon of cricket.

As I say, the remarkable fact about Bradman's batsmanship is its steady observance of the unities. At Leeds he was credited with the invention of a new kind of hook. But there was no scope at Leeds for any sort of hook, ancient or modern. The ball never rose stump high on the first day; how can any batsman hook a ball that does not rise at a sharp angle from the ground? I have never yet seen Bradman perform the hook stroke, but I have seen him pull often enough. The pull, indeed, is one of his most efficient hits; it is timed to perfection, and the sound of it is as sweet as a nut.

At Leeds more than half of his 46 fours were drives in front of the wicket. His drive and cut, indeed, were much more frequently to be seen than his pull and leg hit. The secret of his stroke-power lies in his ability to move quickly backwards or forwards, making the length short or overpitched. The area of the wicket wherein a ball can be pitched that is a good length to Bradman is considerably narrower than that which is defended by all our county batsmen, Woolley excepted. He judges the direction of the attack rapidly; never is he to be seen lunging forward, stretched speculatively out; never does he fall into that 'two-minded' state which compels a batsman to make 'A-shaped bridges down the wicket feeling awry in the air for the ball,' to quote C. B. Fry. Bradman clinches Fry's celebrated Fallacy of Reach:

> The Fallacy of Reach is fatal to true cricket. None but a giant by advancing the left foot and pushing out down the wicket can reach within feet of the pitch of a good length slow ball or within yards of the pitch of a good length fast ball. Why, the very thing the bowler wants one to do, what he works to make one do, is to feel forward at the pitch of his bowling.

Bradman plays back or else goes the whole way of the forcing stroke on punitive decisive feet, When he is as a last resort compelled to play forward, he actually goes back on his wicket to do so, and his legs are behind the bat, and his eyes are on the ball. So strong is his back play, and so quick his eyes and feet, that it is fatal to bowl a short length to him. Yet, so far, that is the mistake the English bowlers have made against Bradman. Frankly they have not stood up to his punishment. Flattered by everyday batsmanship (right foot rooted behind the crease), English bowling has wilted at the sight of a bat that is busy and resolute; hence an attempt to take refuge in short bowling, a safe enough dodge in front of a cricketer who cannot cut. Bradman has thriven on bowling which he has been at liberty to see all the way, to see pitch yards in front of him.

If he has a weak point, Robins, by accident or design, found it out occasionally at Trent Bridge. Every time (which was not often) that Robins sent a well-flighted ball to Bradman, pitched on the middle stump and spinning away, Bradman was observed to be thinking hard, entirely on the defensive. It is not, of course, for the pavilion critic to presume to know the way that Bradman can be got out cheaply. But it is surely not presumptuous for anybody to suggest that the short-pitched ball is about the last of all to send to a batsman with Bradman's voracious appetite for fours and his range of hits.

He has all the qualities of batsmanship: footwork, wrists, economy of power, the great strokes of the game, each thoroughly under control. What, then, is the matter with him that we hesitate to call him a master of style, an artist who delights us, and not only a craftsman we are bound to admire without reserve? Is it that he is too mechanically faultless for sport's sake? A number of Bradmans would quickly put an end to the glorious uncertainty of cricket. A number of Macartneys would inspire the game to hazardous heights more exhilarating than ever. . . . But this is a strain of criticism that is comically churlish. Here have we been for years praying for a return of batsmanship to its old versatility and aggression; we have been desperate for the quick scorer who could hit fours without causing the game to lapse into the indiscriminate clouting of the village green. In short, we have been crying out for batsmanship that would combine technique and energy in proportion.

And now that a Bradman has come to us, capable of 300 runs in a single day of a Test match, some of us are calling him a Lindrum of cricket. It is a hard world to please. Perhaps by making a 'duck' some day, Bradman will oblige those of his critics who believe with Lord Bacon that there should always be some strangeness, something unexpected, mingled with art and beauty.

Grimmett

He is an unobtrusive little man, with a face that says nothing to you at all; seldom is he heard by the crowd when he appeals for leg-before-wicket. He walks about the field on dainty feet which step as though with the soft fastidiousness of a cat treading a wet pavement. He is a master of surreptitious arts; he hides his skill, and sometimes, when he is on guard at cover, he seems to hide himself. He knows a trick of getting himself unobserved, and he darts forward to run a man out like somebody emerging from an ambush.

'Gamp is my name and Gamp my nature.' That is a dark metaphysical saying; the meaning cannot be put into words, but none the less we can grasp it by the instinct for eternal substances. It is like that with Grimmett; the name penetrates to the quiddity, like 'curl', 'twist', 'slithery'; his name is onomatopoeic. I love to see him bowl a man out behind his back, so to say – round the legs; the ball gently touches the stumps and removes perhaps only one bail. The humorous cunning of it reminds me that the Artful Dodger used to walk stealthily behind his master and extract the handkerchief from the coat-tails without Fagin's ever noticing it. Compare Grimmett with the wonderful leg-spin bowler he succeeded in the Australian eleven, Arthur Mailey. An Australian once said to me: 'Mailey bowled the googly stuff like a millionaire; "Clarrie" bowls it like a miser.' Mailey tossed up his spin with all the blandness in the world; his full-tosses were like a generous sort of fattening diet – before the killing and the roasting. Mailey did his mischief by daylight. Grimmett goes to work with a dark lantern; his boots are rubbered. Mailey's wickets were like a practised and jolly angler's 'catch'; Grimmett's wickets are definitely 'swag'. When he goes off the field after he has had 7 for 57, I can see the bag he is carrying over his shoulder.

He is the greatest right-handed spin-bowler of our period. The comparison with Mailey was employed to stress not resemblance but difference; Grimmett is less a 'googly' than a leg-break bowler. He uses the 'wrong' one sparsely; he is content to thrive on the ball which breaks away and leaves the bat; that is the best of all balls. A straight ball, wickedly masked, is Grimmett's foil to the leg-break. He makes a virtue of a low arm; his flight keeps so close to the earth that only a batsman quick of foot can jump to the pitch of it. And then must he beware of Oldfield, the wicket keeper who stumps you with courtesy; he does not make a noise to the umpire, but almost bows you from the wicket. Or he is like a perfect dentist who says when your heart is in your mouth: 'It's all over; I've already got it out; here it is.' To play forward to Grimmett, to miss the spin, and then to find yourself stumped by Oldfield – why, it is like an amputation done under an anaesthetic.

Moments come to all of us when we are uplifted beyond the ordinary; we become touched with grace for a while; we become vessels of inspiration. Felicity descended on Grimmett at Trent Bridge in June 1930, on the first day of the Test match. I have never seen cleverer bowling on a good wicket against great players. Hammond was batting; he made two of his own great forcing off-side hits, off the back foot. These strokes told us that Hammond was in form. Grimmett bowled him a straight ball which sped sinfully from the beautiful turf. Hammond lbw to Grimmett. Next came Woolley. Left-handed batsmen love leg-spin bowlers: the break turns the ball inwards to the middle of the bat. But Grimmett did not send a leg-break to Woolley: he sent the 'googly', whipping away. Woolley's forward stroke was seduced by the fulsome length. Woolley was stumped by Oldfield. A few minutes afterwards Grimmett drew Hendren a yard out of his crease like a mesmerist; then, having got Hendren where he wanted him, not far enough down the pitch, but yet too far, he bowled him. Grimmett will remember in his old age how he spun and 'floated' the ball that day; by the chimney corner he will babble of the way he turned a batsman's smooth lawn into a 'sticky dog'. By sheer craftsmanship he overthrew three great batsmen; nothing to intimidate, no brute force (as George Lohmann called fast bowling of sorts); nothing but a slow spinning ball bowled by a little man with an arm as low as my grandfather's.

The first sight of Grimmett bowling arouses mild laughter. His action recalls the ancient round-arm worthies, or it recalls cricket on the sands with a walking stick for the wicket and a father of six playing for the first time for years. A few steps, a shuffle, and Grimmett's arm seems to creak, But watch his wrist and his fingers: they are sinuous and beautiful. The wrist twirls and swivels; the fingers seem to adore and caress the ball, with the touch of a parent. Grimmett's fingers are always light and wonderfully tactile; when he passes the salt at dinner he imparts the 'fluence'.

He is, I believe, a sign-writer by profession. Can't you see his right wrist at work, sweeping the brush along the ornamentation? Can't you see the fingers intimately putting the finishing flick to a full-stop? Or can't you see the skeleton key at work, finding the way through the locked door of Sutcliffe's bat? He is, as I say, a master of surreptitious arts. His countenance expresses no joy when he confounds his opponents. But I imagine that long after close of play, as he lies in bed and thinks about it, he laughs far into the night. That apparent half-volley which Walters tried to drive; that obvious long-hop that Hendren tried to hook. Confidence tricks! O my lungs and liver, the wickedness of the world!

He seldom gets a man caught in the deep field. That is an

open and a brazen way to rifle the English house. Better by far a swift catch at first slip, or at the wicket best of all lbw; nobody knows anything about it away from the scene of the burglary. He is a great character, not only a great bowler. Sometimes he fancies himself as a batsman. He thrusts his left foot across and drives. Or he waits for it and cuts elegantly. Occasionally he plays late and sees his stumps all awry. Then, and only then, does he wear his heart on his sleeve.

Everybody cherishes private ambitions; we all wish to be what we are not. Dan Leno sighed to play Hamlet; Henry Irving enjoyed himself best when he sat on his top hat and pretended to be Jingle in a farce derived from *Pickwick*. Grimmett made fifty in a Test match at Nottingham in June; perhaps in his old age he will remember Trent Bridge not for his great bowling of 1930, but for his preposterously stylish and first-class half-century of 1934. The rest of the world will dwell for ever on his spin, learned in Australia, where a slow bowler must do his own work and not depend on nature and friendly wickets.

For my part I shall think of him always as I saw him at Worcester in May, taking the county's last wicket and winning the game. A catch was missed from him, and in the same over another lofty chance was skied near cover. Grimmett would trust nobody but Grimmett this time; he ran after the ball himself, and when he caught it he put it in his pocket and glided from the field, concealed entirely amongst ten other victorious Australians.

The Ashes 1936–37:
On the *Orion* to Australia

Life on the ship during the voyage out was not according
to my expectations; I began it with some romantic ideas
lingering in my mind since my boyhood about the talks
and intimacy which would occur amongst a company
of cricketers setting forth to play Australia. The team
merged with the rest of the passengers until you scarcely
knew where they were or which was which; Allen rightly
encouraged his men temporarily to avoid cricket. The fun
of the voyage was at times not easily to be marked off from
the fun of a fashionable hotel on any evening at Folkestone
after a day at the September festival. It became boring, and
I gladly escaped from it. I even left the captain's table – not
disrespectfully, I hope. The captain was charming and a
marvel of tact. But the time arrived when I was ready either
to laugh outright or become sarcastic at the efforts of the
social climbers who each evening vied with one another to

obtain the captain's recognition. The snobbishness on an ocean-going liner is appalling. I imagine that most captains in the service would like at times to leave the captain's table. But this is another digression.

When we reached the Red Sea, I decided to begin a diary; I did not keep it up, of course, for the simple reason that on a ship nothing often happens, Mark Twain achieved the perfect summary:

Oct. 13, Got up, washed, went to bed.
  " 14, "   " "   "   " "
  " 15, "   " "   "   " "

and so on and so forth.

My own entries are a little fuller; here they are:

September 25

'Passengers may sleep on deck in the vicinity of the forward lounge between midnight and 6.30 a.m.' – so runs, with much confidence, the notice that has today been given prominence in the various premises of the *Orion*. We are in the Red Sea as I write, and there is scarcely a soul on board, not including the ship's cat, who is capable of any form of sleep, either on deck or below the deck, in cabin or under the starry heavens; the Red Sea is at its hottest, its stickiest, its cruellest. There is no air in the world, except fetid breath from the desert; the *Orion* makes not a wisp of a breeze as she goes her patient course. The sun is merciless, and when we escape the chastisement of its fiery rods by going under awnings or inside the lounge or drawing-room or tavern or café, then we are suffocated, or, rather, put under some evil drug of the Orient. There is one place only where we can find momentary release from the torment – in the dining-room (only we don't want to dine), where the atmosphere is marvellously chilled. Here the temperature is 75 degrees, and as we enter it we feel as though we have gone into a refrigerator; we expect, even hope, to see frost and snow appearing over our bodies. When at last we reluctantly leave the dining room and pass out through its swing doors, we go straight, without a second's break, into an oven.

I have never before dreamed that the world could become so hot, that people could endure such miseries, that nature could go its ways so indifferent to mortal needs. For three days the sun has hurled down on us the light and heat that destroys; for three days the sky has contained not a cloud, nothing but the pitiless blue of endless and indifferent space. And hour by hour the sea has grown hotter, so that at night, after the sun has gone down and a lovely silver horn of a moon has enchanted the sky, even then we have had no peace, for the waters hold the day's scorchings and throw them back. 'Passengers may sleep on deck' – may, indeed! I did not try; I kept to my cabin and hopefully manipulated the device that blows air upon you, risking sore throat, stiff neck, double pneumonia. Anything would be better and more merciful than to 'pass out' from Red Sea humidity, either by oozing away or by going mad and diving overboard with such despair that one hit the floor of the ocean and perished as much from concussion of the brain as from drowning.

The other evening, a quarter of an hour before dinner, I met Captain Howard on the staircase; the manager of the MCC team had only ten minutes ago changed into his dinner jacket. His collar was already a rag; Mr. Gladstone, after four hours or so of eloquence, never more drastically reduced stiff linen to this state of shapeless wetness. From the foreheads of all of us waterfalls have descended, splashing and dashing like the cascades of Southey's poem. (Was it Southey? – it is still too hot to think here, though at last we are emerging from the Red Sea and a breeze is stirring, giving us a sense of resurrection of all the world from the dead.) At the first hint of this heaven-sent zephyr R. W. V. Robins stripped off his evening jacket and, regardless of dignity and braces, went to the promenade deck and, feeling the faintest suggestion of a wind, said to me: 'We seem to be cooling as we direct our course towards the Antarctic'. Robins has suffered much and has borne it all with humour and an Alfred Lester sort of fortitude.

Everything that science can do towards the defeat of the Red Sea is done on the *Orion*, but nature, as Mr Squeers said, is a 'rum 'un'. 'She's a lovely ship,' said Hammond, 'but I wish she – well, had wings!' I tell of these hardships not out of a desire to present ourselves as martyrs and heroes but to console those we have left at home on the brink of an English winter. 'Lucky you!' they said as we departed from Southampton a fortnight ago; 'oh, lucky, to be going into the sunshine, while we shiver in the east winds and hug our hot-water bottles!' At the moment of writing, there is scarcely an English man or woman on the boat who would not cheerfully give pounds and pounds sterling for one hour of Manchester's wettest rain and coldest cold. Happy days are probably waiting for us in Australia – we shall deserve them, for we have suffered in the Red Sea's cauldron.

But such is human nature that while we were writhing and dissolving in the Red Sea, we persuaded ourselves that the Red Sea was really behaving with unusual moderation; then the moment we sniffed a wind of the Indian Ocean we agreed unanimously that the Red Sea had broken records in heat and life-destroying humidity, and we went about amongst ourselves distributing medals for patience, endurance, and philosophy, so to say. The probability is that we revealed ourselves as so many comfortable creatures of the temperate zone of the earth; it is said by the knowing ones of these parts that the more intelligent inhabitants of the Nubian Desert sometimes visit the Red Sea to enjoy its bracing climate – to them the Red Sea is the Skegness of the Tropics.

Pleasures there have been for us, of course; lazy days in the Mediterranean, when the sunshine has been friendly and the swimmers in the bathing-pool have splashed about, before stretching themselves luxuriously in the lovely slanting light of the late afternoon. Then the evenings. First the sunsets, and the peacefulness that comes over the ship before dinner; people have retired to dress, and the solitary watcher, leaning on the ship's side, has the sense for a moment that he is being divested of personal identity and absorbed into the deepening beauty of the hour of twilight over the ocean as the evening star appears. At night the dancing begins, and here again it is good to escape from the glitter and animation, to withdraw and watch from a point apart. Then it is possible to feel the pathos of contrast – the light and happy intimacy of life brought together for a moment by chance; and the surrounding and lasting immensity of the Indian Ocean.

And while all the laughter of young people goes on, and the elders sit domestically in lounge and drawing-room enjoying familiar comforts, the ship moves on, a beautiful sensitive creature, with the flexibility of a canoe and the power and grandeur of an ocean-going liner; through the night it moves, throbbing with a poised life of its own, making a wake in the water delicate as a chain.

At the moment we are well beyond Aden, a sun-cursed pile of brown rock, oleaginous, with the refuse kites flapping in the air – a place where the White Man's Burden, and the Black Man's Burden too, can be felt as a weariness to flesh and spirit. We are following the track of a monsoon, and the ship is rolling. In the middle of the night it is thrilling for the landsman to listen from his cabin to the surge outside, and to feel the whole of the boat's nervous system working; you can hear the heart of it. I have grown to love the ship and the quiet certainty of the men who control its strength, grace, and nobility.

October 17

. . . Life on a ship is concentrated in so small a space that in a month a man exceeds the common length of days. The distractions and responsibilities of the world come for a while to an end; as the hours go by we can almost count each pulsation of existence; consciousness and sense of personal identity become pure and absolute. And a strange sort of pathos falls on the little world we make for ourselves during the voyage; we know it cannot last long, that friendships almost certainly will come to an end soon, that all our efforts to reproduce the world we have left on land must end in irony – yet we do indeed reproduce it, I am afraid, with as many as possible of its foibles and pretensions. We live as though in a bubble which we have ourselves blown up, and as the voyage goes on the more does the bubble swell to bursting-point.

I have loved the evenings sitting in the 'Tavern' before dinner, watching the swimmers in the bathing-pool while the sun sank over the Indian Ocean and the sky turned to a sudden purple and stars appeared as though kindled one by one. I loved the careless fun of the games deck, the fun with the children in their own playground. I loved to go at half-past ten every morning into what I called the 'Market Place', because it was there that C. B. Fry held court amongst the deck-chairs and the passing life of the ship; where we discussed all things under the sun. Perhaps our arguments were rather too contrapuntal to be easily followed by the listening throng; we each went our way, talking for art's sake, keeping count of our own bull's eyes. But one day, just to tease him, I said: 'Well, Charles, good morning. No hemlock yet? Give us your views on the origin of the Iambic.' It was a pure piece of banter; the word 'Iambic' came to my mind by the merest chance. I might as well have asked him to explain the origin of King Cole or green cabbages.

But Fry, without a moment's hesitation, launched into a remarkable piece of virtuoso exposition; in half an hour he sketched, with a swift touch and comprehensive illustrative detail, the history of prosody. And he had not finished when I left him and went for my morning walk seven times round the deck, making the mile. Each time I passed the ship's centre (the 'Market Place') he was still at it – 'You see what I mean? However . . .' He wore a confusing variety of clothes day by day, clothes of strange dyes, patterns, and purposes. Only once did he appear (save at dinner) in tolerably reasonable guise, and that was at a fancy-dress ball, when he simulated an ascetic yet genial scoutmaster. The next day he wore what I called his deep-sea fishing attire, and I said: 'Glad to see you back in fancy dress, Charles'.

The team went quietly about their pleasures. Verity read *Seven Pillars of Wisdom* from beginning to end. Hammond won at all games, from chess to deck quoits. Maurice Leyland smoked his pipe, and Duckworth danced each evening with a nice understanding of what, socially, he was doing. Wyatt took many photographs and developed them himself. Fry, armed with a most complicated camera, also took many photographs, and none of them could be developed.

After we left Colombo the heat mercifully cooled down and a fresh wind blew. We came upon the Cocos Islands suddenly on a windy morning. Never shall I forget the romantic beauty of this experience. All the adventure stories of my youth sprang to life; here was Stevenson, Ballantyne, Defoe. On the little beach, silent and empty, there was surely Man Friday's footprint; the colours on the water evoked visions of enchanted lagoons, treasure, and coral. In a towering sea two little boats came bravely to take a barrel from the *Orion* containing the quarterly supply of rations for the handful of men who work on the islands, supporting the Empire and the White Man's Burden. The barrel was taken on board, and mighty waves swept past the two boats, sometimes hiding them from our view. On the *Orion* we all leaned over the side and waved farewell. And the last we saw of the little boats was their plungings and swayings as they returned to the island, with the men waving farewell in return; there was not a person on board the *Orion* who did not feel the emotion of the scene. 'It makes a lump come into your throat,' said William Voce of Nottinghamshire.

When we reached Fremantle it was seven in the morning. We had to be up and about early. Many times on the voyage I had wakened in the dawn and looked through my porthole. There is magic in things seen from a ship's porthole; it becomes a magic mirror. I saw the sunrise on the Indian Ocean through my porthole, and felt ashamed to be prying into an act of beauty so secret and removed from human interference. Through my porthole I saw Australia for the first time.

When Cricket Changed

For twenty years I went to cricket matches north, south, east and west, and I saw the blossom come upon orchards in Gloucestershire, as we journeyed from Manchester to Bristol; and I saw midsummer in full blaze at Canterbury; and I saw midsummer dropping torrents of rain on the same lovely place, the white tents dropsical: 'Play abandoned for the day.' I saw the autumn leaves falling at Eastbourne. I have shivered to the bone in the springtime blasts at the Parks at Oxford. In a *Manchester Guardian* article I congratulated the keenness and devotion of two spectators who at Leicester sat all day, near the sightscreen, from eleven until half-past six, in spite of an east wind like a knife. Then, as I was finishing my notice, a thought struck me. 'But', I added in a final sentence, 'perhaps they were only dead.'

I have seen English summer days pass like a dream as the cricketers changed places in the field over by over.

Sometimes I have seen in vision all the games going on throughout the land at the same minute of high noon; Hobbs, easy and unhurriedly on the way to another hundred under the gasometer at the Oval; Tate and Gilligan at Hove skittling wickets while the tide comes in; Hendren and Hearne batting for ever at Lord's while the Tavern gets busier and busier; at Southampton, Kennedy bowling for hours for Hampshire – Kennedy never ceased bowling in those days; he could always have produced a clinching alibi if ever circumstantial evidence had convicted him of anything:

'What were you doing on July 17th at four forty-five in the afternoon?'

'Why, bowling of course.'

From Old Trafford to Dover, from Hull to Bristol, the fields were active as fast bowlers heaved and thudded and sweated over the earth, and batsmen drove and cut or got their legs in front; and the men in the slips bent down, all four of them together, as though moved by one string. On every afternoon at half-past six I saw them, in my mind's eye, all walking home to the pavilion, with a deeper tan on their faces. And the newspapers came out with the cricket scores and the visitor from Budapest, in London for the first time, experienced a certain bewilderment when he saw an *Evening News* poster: 'Collapse of Surrey'.

In these twenty seasons I saw also a change in cricket. It is not fanciful, I think, to say that a national game is influenced by the spirit and atmosphere of the period. In

1920 cricket retained much of the gusto and free personal gesture of the years before the war of 1914-1918. Then, as disillusion increased and the nation's life contracted and the catchword 'safety first' became familiar and a sense of insecurity gathered, cricket itself lost confidence and character.

My own county of Lancashire provided a striking example of how a mere game can express a transition in the social and industrial scene. When Manchester was wealthy and the mills of Lancashire were busy most days and nights, cricket at Old Trafford was luxuriant with Maclaren, Spooner and Tyldesley squandering runs opulently right and left. It was as soon as the county's shoe began to pinch and mill after mill closed, that Lancashire cricket obtained its reputation for suspicious thriftiness; care and want batted visibly at both ends of the wicket. Not that the players consciously expressed anything; of course they didn't. But a cricketer, like anybody else, is what his period and environment make of him, and he acts or plays accordingly.

The romantic flourish vanished as much from cricket as from the theatre and the arts. I even reacted against the romanticism in my own cricket writing. The lyric gush, the 'old flashing bat' and 'rippling green grass' metaphors gave way to, or became tinctured with, satire if not with open irony. Hammond no longer inspired me into comparisons between him and the Elgin marbles; I saw something middle-class and respectable about his play, and was vastly amused and relieved when occasionally he fell off his pedestal and struck a ball with the oil-hole of his bat, or received a blow from a fast ball on his toe.

Bradman was the summing-up of the Efficient Age which succeeded the Golden Age. Here was brilliance safe and sure, streamlined and without impulse. Victor Trumper was the flying bird; Bradman the aeroplane. It was the same in music, by the way: the objective Toscanini was preferred to the subjective Furtwängler. In an England XI of 1938, A. C. Maclaren would have looked as much an anachronism as Irving in a Noel Coward play.

Interlude: 'That Means War'

I have looked into an account I wrote of a journey from Manchester I went upon to write about cricket:

Observe, happy man, from your bedroom window, at this moment as you prepare yourself for a journey to the South, observe the passers-by along the street opposite. They are going to work, going to the city, there to live stuffily in one dingy spot, while you-while you are going away for the beginning of a new cricket season. Tonight these same poor souls will pass by your house again, back from the city, but you will not be there to see them return. By then you will be at the other end of England; perhaps you will have just been taken by the hotel porter to your room, just have unpacked, washed and gone out into the delicious streets, to delight yourself in them with the feeling of the miles you have covered that day . . .

At Wellington [continues this diary of a pilgrim-age], or in some such place deep in the garden of our land, the journey is broken; there is a change here. The Manchester train goes out, leaving you exquisitely aware that you are now quite out of touch with Manchester. Your connection arrives – a train that obviously has never been in Manchester. The people on it have just as obviously never been in Manchester. Here, unmis-takably, you are in a fresh hemisphere, entering on the last lap of your journey, through a drowsy landscape. And how peaceful is the closing hour of a day's railway travel; the mild agitations of the morning have spent themselves. The senses are tired at last of responding to new scenes, new sounds, new odours . . .

Anybody reading that passage in cold blood might imagine that I had travelled on a magic carpet, to realms of gold, over minaret and hanging gardens. If I am not mistaken I had gone to Kidderminster to watch Worcester v Lancashire. I confess that when I journeyed from England to Australia by air, on the most marvel-lous of magic carpets, one you could dine on, and have an excellent hock for lunch, I was not once inspired to such an Odyssey as the one described above, written in 1921. 'Delicious streets', you will observe. Perhaps they were delicious, a quarter of a century ago. I saw them in time, whether streets of Kidderminster, Worcester, Canterbury, Leicester, Taunton, Tonbridge, Gloucester or Ashby de la

Zouch – I saw them looking far from delicious, as the last rays from the summer evening sunshine fell like naphtha on pavements full of pimply youths in thirty-shilling suits and suede shoes, with their girlfriends, nearly all bad of tooth, either going into or coming out of a Palais de Danse or Plaza.

And the inns and hotels where I unpacked and washed in subsequent years: the same can for hot water, the same night commode with a tin clasp, the same wardrobe that came open suddenly after resistance, the same dressing-table with signs on the top of it that some former guest had been careless with his cigarettes, the same glass and water-bottle, and the same sickly pink counterpane. And in the breakfast-room next morning, the same cloistered dyspeptic gloom, and fried eggs like baleful yellow eyes, and the same resigned waiters. It was an England day by day losing character and all joy in life generated by the individual. It was an England becoming more and more unfriendly and shut up in itself and resigned.

Even at cricket matches in these country towns, I often felt a sense of dejection. The local caterer supplied the lunches for the crowds at a good profit, poor feeble stuff washed down by bottled beer brought miles. The people sometimes hardly seemed to possess strength to cheer boundary hits, when at intervals they happened. The last time I sat on the rustic benches of Taunton cricket field in summer, I watched two Somersetshire professionals, both entirely of the town clerkly, pushing and poking their bats

at spiritless long-hops and half volleys. And I imagined
the ghost of Sammy Woods looking on helpless to get at
the bowling.

I came before long to dislike these miasmas of urban
monotony. There was at least character at Old Trafford
and Sheffield. But at last I made Lord's my headquarters,
though never a member of the MCC and never free to go
into the pavilion during a Test match except by special dis-
pensation. Lord's conceded to the march of progress only
on her own terms, holding the balance between tradition
and change. The tulips were brought up to wear the MCC
colours. I always felt that the MCC did not in its heart of
hearts approve of a big crowd present at Lord's. When rain
fell at Lord's, putting an end to play for hours, the crowd
was in God's good time informed whether further cricket
would take place that day; a man was sent round the field
propelling a contraption on wheels, like a velocipede, carrying a board on which were chalked some tidings from
the captains or the umpires as to their intentions and the
state of the wicket.

I have known Australians to visit Lord's for the first
time and loathe the feeling they received there of custom
and prerogative. But after a while I have known the same
Australians thoroughly assimilated, in love with the old
order it stood for; they became more royal than the King.
They enjoyed seeing the patricians in the Long Room at
lunch, eating meat pies and drinking cans of beer-like
patricians. Lord's was not, of course, all school-tie and

patrician; it was a microcosm of London itself. There was
the East End-near the Tavern — as well as the West End of
the Long Room. When the promenade on the grass took
place during lunch, Seven Dials was free to move with
Belgrave Square; a Hendren is as symbolical of Lord's as
ever the Hon. C. N. Bruce. Still, there is a limit to things;
you can have J. W. Hearne at Lord's a sort of butler; you can
have Patsy a head-groom or coachman; you can have big
genial Jim Smith, out of the garden, so to say, or something to do with the buttery. But at Lord's you could not in
decency have an Emmott Robinson permanently on the
premises or any other embodiment of industry or trade.
Cricket, I say, honours the *habitat*; the social historian will
find in a study of it and its environment much that the blue
books omit.

A hundred times I have walked down the St John's Wood
Road on a quiet morning – that's the proper way to enjoy
Lord's: choose a match of no importance, for preference
one for which the fixture card promises a 'band if possible'. I have gone a hundred times into the Long Room
out of the hot sun and never have I not felt that this is a
good place to be in, and if the English simply *had* to make
cricket a national institution and a passion and a pride,
this was the way to do it, in a handsome hall and pavilion,
a resting-place for the game's history, with its constitution
to be found as much in *Debrett* as in *Wisden*. I have looked
through the great windows on the field of play and seen the
cricketers in the heat, moving like creatures in another

element, the scene as though suspended in time; the crowd a painted canvas; the blue sky and the green of the trees at the nursery end; the lordly ones slumbering on the white seats of the pavilion, or quietly talking.

On the Friday morning when Hitler invaded Poland, I chanced to be in this same Long Room at Lord's watching through windows for the last time for years. Though no spectators were present, a match was being continued; there was no legal way of stopping it. Balloon barrages hung over Lord's. As I watched the ghostly movements of the players outside, a beautifully preserved member of Lord's, spats and rolled umbrella, stood near me inspecting the game. We did not speak of course; we had not been introduced. Suddenly two workmen entered the Long Room in green aprons and carrying a bag. They took down the bust of W. G. Grace, put it into the bag, and departed with it. The noble lord at my side watched their every movement; then he turned to me. 'Did you see, sir?' he asked.

I told him I had seen.

'That means war,' he said.

The Roses Match

On Saturday next I shall go to Leeds to watch the forty-second match since the war between Lancashire and Yorkshire; the occasion will complete my twenty-first year as a commentator in this paper on the greatest of all tussles between county rivals.

In most matches the critic endeavours to be impartial; he sits aloft in the press-box, like an impersonal god, seeing all things moving, towards their predestined end. The Lancashire and Yorkshire match is an exception; I step down from the pedestal of impartiality. I become for a few days as prone as anybody else in the crowd to the passions of the partisan. If two Yorkshire batsmen make a long stand (and if one of them happens to be Arthur Mitchell by name and by nature) I do my best to exert an influence of will over the field of play – some current of hate and malice calculated to cause mishap, if not death and destruction, to take place at the wicket for the benefit of my native county.

I have found that a partnership can often be broken by leaving the press box and retiring for a moment (usefully) behind the scene. I have this way taken a hundred wickets for Lancashire in twenty-one successive seasons.

The mind holds events in these games vividly; they remain coloured by imagination in a frieze of memory, set against a grim and humorous background of North of England life. No other match expresses so much character. The crowd is part of the whole; it exults and it suffers – especially does it suffer. A year or two ago Lancashire defeated Yorkshire somehow at Sheffield. When the winning hit was about to be made, when the fact became clear that no power on earth could save Yorkshire, a man wearing a cloth cap was sitting miserably amongst the litter on the great and forbidding mound which stands one side of the ground. And his wife said to him: 'Well, tha would come, wouldn't thi?'

Many years ago another Lancashire victory happened at Leeds in surprising circumstances. On August Bank Holiday Lancashire, according to long custom, collapsed. I wrote severely about the weak play exhibited by our batsmen. Next morning Yorkshire needed only a few runs to win, and everybody thought they would get them without the loss of a wicket. We turned up at Headingley merely as a matter of form. I believe that Emmott Robinson resented having to go through the ritual of changing into flannels. 'Waste o' time and money,' he probably said. Yorkshire collapsed incredibly, and Lancashire won by some twenty runs. That evening I received an anonymous postcard from a patriot who had read my diatribe on Lancashire's batting; it was brief and to the point, but not entirely fit for publication: 'You——— fool,' it said; simply that and nothing more.

I shall remember all my life the finish of this match. After Yorkshire's last wicket fell I rushed from the Headingley ground and got on a tram, eager to carry the good news, hot from the burning, to Manchester. The tram guard came jauntily to me for my fare; he was whistling. 'What ha' they won by?' he asked.

I said, 'They haven't won; they've lost.'

He replied, 'Ah mean t' cricket match – did they lose any wickets?'

When I assured him I had referred to t'cricket match, and that Yorkshire really had been defeated he suspended business on the spot; he did not give me a ticket, but turned his back on me and walked to the front of the tram, where he opened the door and told the driver. Then the tram proceeded a mile or so into Leeds by its own volition.

In Leeds the dreadful news had travelled before me; you could see the effect on most faces. I went to the railway station, and as my train would not come for half an hour I entered the refreshment room. Shortly a few of the crowd dribbled in, sadly returning home. A Yorkshireman sat down at my table. He looked at me and said, 'Hey, this is a reight do. Fancy Yorkshire put out for fifty. Ah thowt better of them.' There was no anger in his voice, only sorrow.

Then he looked at me again, harder. 'Tha doesn't seem to be takin' it to 'eart very much,' he said.

I told him that, as I was from Lancashire, I naturally could not see the disaster from his point of view.

He inspected me now from a different angle. 'Oh,' he said, 'so tha comes from Lancashire?'

Once more I admitted that I did.

'And tha come specially to see t' finish this mornin'?'

I answered in the affirmative.

'Ah suppose tha's feelin' pleased with thisen?'

I did not deny it.

'And tha's goin' back to Manchester by this two-twenty train?'

Yes, I said, I was.

'Goin' back reight now?'

Yes, I reiterated.

'Well,' he said, slowly and in measured terms, 'Ah 'opes tha drops down dead before thi gets theer.'

There is no crowd in the world to equal the Lancashire and Yorkshire cricket crowd. Sutcliffe once stonewalled at Old Trafford for half an hour, almost without scoring. The afternoon was warm, and a huge multitude sat in silence. The game seemed to become suspended out of time and space. Nothing disturbed the illusion of eternity. Suddenly a voice addressed Sutcliffe, not critically, but with simple, honest inquiry: "Erbert,' the voice solicited, "Erbert, coom on; what dost tha think thi are, a ——— war memorial?'

In August, 1919, the first season after the war, two-day county matches were played, and at Sheffield on the Tuesday after Bank Holiday Hallows batted from noon till evening and saved the match for Lancashire. The crowd worked hard to get him out. Twenty thousand of them emitted a staccato noise as soon as each ball bowled at Hallows left the bowler's hand. 'Hoo!' they said (I cannot find an onomatopoeic sign eloquent enough). At six o'clock the crowd gave up the bad job and began to leave the trying scene. Rhodes vainly sought to tempt Hallows, but Hallows continued to push the ball away with his own stately ease and insolence.

A solitary man remained on the mound. He was black in the face. All the afternoon he had done his utmost with his 'Hoo!' Rhodes bowled the last over of the day. The lonely man on the mound let out six desperate 'Hoo's!' The final one exploded in the darkening air. Hallows patted the last ball of the last over, and the players began to leave the field. The man on the mound surveyed Hallows, gathered together all his remaining energy and passion, and howled forth, 'Oh, ——— you!' and went home.

Walter Hammond

Walter Hammond was one of the truly great cricketers
in the game's history; it would be hard to leave him out
of any recorded England XI, though blasphemy might
be committed if we altered a single name of the mag-
nificent membership of the England XI which played at
Birmingham in 1902; who of these could with justice and
decency stand down even for Hammond – A. C. MacLaren,
C. B. Fry, K. S. Ranjitsinhji, F. S. Jackson, Tyldesley, Lilley,
Hirst, G. L. Jessop, Braund, Lockwood, Rhodes? Do I hear
a whispered suggestion that Tyldesley was not greater than
Hammond as a batsman and no bowler at all? But I cannot
argue reasonably on behalf of J. T. Tyldesley. In his heyday
he was the only English professional player who by batting alone could retain his position in the England team.
I flatter Hammond by bringing his name into contact
with Tyldesley's, even as I honour Tyldesley by the same
verbal conjunction. Hammond indeed was the complete

cricketer in his superb physique, which combined power and lissome movement; his batsmanship attained in time classic poise and the habit of long domination. He was a dangerous medium-paced bowler who, given the ambition, might have vied with George Lohmann in all-round and elegant skill; for I doubt if even Lohmann was Hammond's superior as a slip fieldsman.

He looked the part too, even as Lohmann looked it. His shoulders were broad; the physical frame as a whole maybe at first hinted of top-heaviness somewhere, and there seemed a tendency of his legs, as he stood in the slips, to go together at the knees. At the first sight of a snick from the edge of the bat his energy apparently electrified the shape and substance of him, he became light and bone-less, and down to the earth he would dive, all curves and balance, and he would catch a ghost of a 'chance' as if by instinct; quick though it moved, the body no doubt lagged behind the born gameplayer's intuitions. He could take a slip catch as the ball flashed rapidly away, wheeling on the ballet Lancer's toes and not so much gripping or seizing the ball as bringing it back, so to say, with time to spare. Only A. P. F. Chapman of Hammond's contemporaries equalled Hammond at catching close to the wicket.

I first saw Hammond in 1923 playing against Lancashire Gloucester; he was an unknown youth, and he batted low in the innings, amongst the tail-enders. He drove one four to the off, then got out; but I had seen enough. I wrote half a column in the *Manchester Guardian* about the boy and ventured a prophecy of greatness to come. It was easy to look into his future; there is no mistaking the thorough-bred. We needn't look for hours at quality. The scoreboard and the statisticians must wait for results; and mediocrity needs the proof of print and percentages before it is recognised even as mediocrity. Hammond was born to distinction on the cricket field; before he had been playing Gloucestershire long most of us knew that here was one of the elect, the chosen few. But not everybody knew; in 1924 I argued with John Sharp of Lancashire, then on the England selection committee, that already Hammond was worth his colours. But Sharp thought he lacked discretion; 'He's a bit of a dasher,' he said. In Hammond's career as a batsman can be divided into periods, much as the career of Hobbs can be divided.

First he was all swift aggression, even to the verge of reck-lessness. Then followed the illness which in 1926 nearly put an end to his cricket. And now he merged into maturity just as Test matches were changing in temper and atti-tude according to what I shall herewith call the Jardinian theory, the theory taught by the strongest-willed of all the captains of England Elevens, the theory of the survival not so much of the fittest but of the most durable. The great batsman for the purposes of Test matches, according to this theory, was he who stayed in for hours and compiled large quantities of runs, not necessarily by commanding and beautiful strokes but by the processes of attrition.

Hammond remained to the end a batsman handsome to look at, a pedigree batsman, monumental and classic.

But I shall continue to try to remember well the young Hammond who in 1927, when the Gloucestershire cause seemed lost beyond repair, hooked the pace of MacDonald with a savage power I had seldom seem before and have never seen since. At this point I imagine the eyebrows of most of my more experienced readers are going up questionably – 'Hammond hooking? But Hammond didn't use the hook. If he had a weakness at all it was lack of resourceful strokes to leg. O'Reilly could keep him quiet by bowling on his leg stump.'

On the morning of Friday, 20th May, Gloucestershire, with two wickets down in their second innings, were only 44 ahead. The Lancashire professionals planned to get the match over quickly, so that they could go to the Manchester races. From the first over of the day, bowled by MacDonald with the velocity and concentration of a man determined to get to Castle Irwell in time to back a certain winner at 5 to 1 against, Hammond drove five fours from five consecutive balls. The sixth ball would also have counted for four, but it was fielded on the boundary's edge at the sight-screen behind MacDonald's arm. A straight drive from the first over of the most dangerous fast bowler of many decades! Hammond punished MacDonald so contumaciously that short 'bumpers' soon began whizzing about Hammond's head. He hooked them time after time as ferociously as they were discharged at him. I watched this death-or-glory innings standing in the dusty earth near the Manchester end of the ground, near long leg. Several of Hammond's hooks crashed into the earth, sending gravel flying about us like shrapnel. In some three hours Hammond scored 187, with no chance, four sixes and twenty-four fours.

In August 1924 at the age of 21 he wrecked the Middlesex attack on a dreadful wicket at Bristol. Gloucestershire, in first, scored 31, then dismissed Middlesex for 74. In Gloucestershire's second innings Hammond scored an unbeaten 174 out of 294 for 9 (declared), in four hours, winning the match. It was cricket of this dauntless kind, with strokes blinding to the eyesight, strokes of controlled power and strokes of controlled imagination, all kaleidoscopic and thrilling to the romantic vision, which impelled me to a column article I sent to the *Observer*, then edited by J. L. Garvin, who also became convinced of young Hammond's genius. But we couldn't convince yet the England selection committee that here was the greatest England batsman since the high noon of Hobbs. The philosophy of 'safety first' was at this time in full swing and sway. By the by, when Hammond first got married, Garvin wrote to me: 'For the next few months he'll probably not do very much – but afterwards, better than ever.'

Because of illness Hammond did not play for England until 1927. Then as one of Chapman's team – in Australia in 1928-29 – Jardine, the vice-captain, he scored 905 runs in the rubber, with an average of 113.12. He began modestly in the first Test Match of the series, played at Brisbane:

44 and 28. Next at Sydney he scored 251, followed by 200 and 32 (run out) at Melbourne, followed by 119 not out and 177 at Adelaide (two hundreds in the same game), followed by 38 and 16. The world of cricket was staggered, not realising of the wrath to come from Bradman. So far in cricket's history no one human batsman had amassed runs in Test matches with this insatiable appetite and with Hammond's austerity of purpose and disciplined technique. For he had now put childish things behind him, at least while playing in Test matches. The glorious uncertainty of cricket was a term no longer to be sensibly applied to Test matches between England and Australia; the wickets all this time were anaesthetic, somnolent couches stuffed with runs. We must bear these wickets in mind as we make an estimate of the bowling of W. J. O'Reilly, who was doomed to go to work on them and to toil on them for hours, if he could not spin. In the circumstance his record of performances well bears comparison with that of the unparalleled Sydney Barnes.

Hammond fitted himself into the new economy and the new ethic of sport; and he lost nothing of the grand manner while making the adjustment and the ordered concession to the mathematical and the mechanical. He cut out all but his safest strokes; he became patience on a pedestal of modern concrete; Phoebus Apollo had turned fasting friar. He reserved for matches of lesser importance flashes or flickers of his proper brilliance. His stately and pillared centuries and double-centuries were as classic as the Elgin marbles and about as mobile and substantial. With the ease of absolute mastery he batted maiden over after maiden over, his body bending to the ball almost solicitously, making strokes of cradled gentleness. For the Cause he clipped his own wings; but there is something majestical in wings in repose. He played henceforward mainly off the back foot. His terrific punches to the offside received their strength from a propulsion or a swift thrust of the body beginning at a bent right knee, then steely wrists directed the energy, so that none was wasted; it all ran like a current of power into the bat and through it into the ball.

At Lord's in 1938 his greatest Test match innings may be said to have added to the ground's lustre and history. When he went to the wicket England had lost Hutton, Barnett and Edrich to the alarming pace of McCormick, and not many more than twenty runs had been scored. Hammond at once took charge of the game and after due scrutiny and circum-spection he hammered McCormick and Fleetwood Smith and O'Reilly to shapeless helplessness, never seeming to hurry himself or use his strength combatively; no; he went a red-carpeted way to 240, his cover-drives thundering against the rails under the sign of Father Time.

This innings announced that for Hammond ripeness was all that mattered now; the early and dazzling shooting-star had by some astronomical decree changed into the benign satisfying and fulfilled harvest moon. His batting at Lord's this day was marmoreal; an appeal against him for leg-before wicket, a raucous appeal at that, sounded so incongruous that I was there and then strangely inspired to a satire, in the form of Meredithian parody:

Hammond leg-before-wicket – has anybody noticed that he *has* a leg? Usually the leg of the modern batsman is ever before us, obscure it as you will, dressed degenerately in pads of breadth and length, inordinate unvaried length, sheer longinquity ageing the very heart of bowler on a view. Most cricketers have their legs, we have to admit. But what are they? Not the modulated instrument we mean simply legs for leg-work, legs of an Emmott Robinson. Our cava-lier's leg – our Hammond's is the poetic leg, a valiance, a leg with brains in it, not to be traduced by the trick they ken of at Sheffield . . .

After Hammond put an end to his innings this day in June 1938, everybody stood up as he returned to the pavilion, stood up to render tribute to a cricketer who had ennobled Lord's. After the second war, Hammond again visited Australia, this time as captain. He suffered phys-ical ailment and mental worry, so could not make a good end. But during the 'Victory' Test matches in England, not regarded as official, the original Hammond was seen, riding on the crest of his youth; or, to drop the metaphor, he attacked as of yore, the bat swinging free of care again, sure of aim, and, best of all, a source of enjoyment to himself as well as to all others.

One of his more remarkable innings was played on an absurdly difficult wicket at Melbourne, during the 1936–37 rubber; the ball broke most known laws of geometry, trigonometry and suchlike. Now it shot along the earth like a stone thrown over ice; now from the same length would it rise upward at an acute angle threatening batsman's skull or thorax. On this turbulent pitch Hammond maintained his customary poise and calm; his innings of 32 came like oil in raging waters. He stayed in easefully for an hour and a half, never once obliged to hasten a stroke. The irony of it all was that all this mastery was really a service to Australia; much more good would have come England's way had Hammond driven and hooked, defying every tabulated principle of science, and scored his runs in a quarter of the time – so that Australia might have had to go to the wicket and face the music. J. T. Tyldesley in 1903, also on a foul pitch at Melbourne, made 63 out of England's total of 103, and by brilliance and versatile if sometimes indiscreet strokes, won the match, or at least brought victory within England's reach.

Hammond in his pomp occasionally suggested that he was batting lazily, with not all his mind alert. When he at times scored slowly on a perfect wicket he conveyed to us the impression that he was missing opportunities to get runs because of some absence of mind or indolence of disposition. He once said to me after he had made a large score on a comfortable wicket, 'It's too easy.' He preferred a worn dust-heap at Cheltenham, where he would put the most dangerous attack to the sword, and where fielding in the slips he was Nijinsky and a myriad-armed Indian god at one and the same animate time.

His career had its pungent ironies, apart from the disillusionment of the curtain's fall. When he first met Fleetwood-Smith, a googly bowler of rare and enchanting art, Hammond nearly knocked him out of cricket for good and all. Then in 1937 at Adelaide, when the rubber was at stake, Hammond and Fleetwood-Smith came face to face; and we knew that the decision rested with one or the other. On the closing morning, England needed 244 to win, with 7 wickets in hand, Hammond not out. It was the fourth match of the series, England had won two, Australia one. All our eyes were riveted on Hammond as he took the bowling of Fleetwood-Smith in a gleaming sunshine. To the third ball of the day Hammond played forward and was clean bowled. Australia won, drawing equal in the rubber; they also won the fifth. As Hammond's bails fell to the ground, Fleetwood-Smith danced, walked on his knees, went nearly off his head. And I heard Duckworth's voice behind me: 'We wouldn't have got Don out first thing in the morning with rubber at stake.'

'Too easy.' He was an artist of variable moods. But he was greater than the statisticians suspect. Perhaps all of a beautiful batsman's innings should be of brief duration as Edgar Allen Poe said all poetry should be short. At least no innings by a master and artist should seem longer than any ever played by Trumper, Woolley or John Tyldesley. There were more things in Hammond's cricket than are dreamed of in the scorebook's economy.

The Melbourne Test, 1950, Third Day

This was one of the most astonishing and thrilling days in the annals of cricket, and it ended with the balance so precarious that the merest wisp of a straw from luck would sway it decisively, England's or Australia's way. Yet again Australian batsmanship was rendered poverty-stricken; the second innings was all over at five minutes to five for 181. England counter-attacked grandly from the position to which they were thrown back on Saturday; the wicket, though not altogether after a contemporary batsman's heart, was on the whole true — in spite of a ball that kept low now and again and easy for run-making. Keener bowling than Bedser's, Bailey's and Brown's, and keener fielding, couldn't be imagined; and the raging battle was infused by a spirit of sportsmanship that honoured the finest and oldest traditions of cricket, the Melbourne crowd contributing a generous if ear-shattering part.

After a two days' pause the match began again in hot

weather, the sun streaming from a sky of blue satin stretched without a crease in it. From the heights of the members' pavilion, looking straight down and behind the line of the ball's flight, the wicket resembled a light-brown oblong coffin in which, you might have said, reposed the hopes of all bowlers. But it was a deceptive wicket really good enough for a good batsman, but, as I say, a ball occasionally kept low; and there was always enough hardness in the rolled baked earth to create that illusion in cricket of increase of speed after the ball has pitched. A Test match wicket in Australia, let alone Christmas Day and Boxing Day, could scarcely be expected to remain sober all the time. So once again we were privileged to enjoy a fair fight between bat and ball, fortune never distributing her favours unequally among the opponents.

At first I resigned myself to hours of slow attrition while Morris and Archer set themselves to reduce Bedser, Bailey and Wright to limp, moist, ineffectual bodies. Only one wicket fell before lunch, and in ninety minutes not more than 57 runs were scored; and now Australia were 79 ahead, nine batsmen to come. Morris played back to a well-flighted length from Wright, got into position for a glance to leg, changed his mind, and allowed his pads to stop a 'googly', and to his unconcealed surprise was given out lbw. Still, nobody foresaw the wrath to come. Archer suggested obduracy if not a technical control that has been taught by experience to work at leisure and by instinct.

The fun began at half-past two when the great ground

was packed and inflammable. Archer was caught a few yards from the bat by Bailey, off Bedser in the 'gully', and five minutes afterwards Harvey backed-up impulsively as Miller stabbed defensively forward at a surprisingly quick one from Wright. Washbrook, at mid-off, fielded swiftly, threw at one wicket and struck it with Harvey yards out. I was obliged to ask the brilliant fielder's name; he was so thoroughly disguised in a white hat that he might have been wearing the Tarnhelm. Miller also protected himself from the sun by use of a cap; and Miller with his hair invisible is as though W. G. Grace had appeared without his whiskers.

Indeed, Miller was not happy; his aggression hinted of some mental unease. Clearly the occasion was not going to be a sort of extra Christmas dinner for Australian batsmen. He made two great strokes off Wright, a voracious sweep to leg, the whole man coming full circle, and a leap of a drive to the off. Then Bailey clean-bowled him with dramatic abruptness. Miller tried to change from offence to defence, but the ball's speed was even quicker than Miller's eyesight; the middle stump was hit before the bat could intervene.

Now Brown came into action again, rolling to the crease like a man-of-war. A rasping ball removed Loxton, caught at the wicket: Australia 5 for 131, and what with the boiling temperature of the afternoon and the roars and the zoological screams of the women in the crowd, the wonder is that typewriters in the Press Box were not dislocated and infinitives split asunder. The frenzy of it all was intensified by the impersonal tranquillity of the stainless blue sky. Brown next got rid of Lindwall, also caught at the wicket; and in the same over Brown, insatiable and very warm, defeated Tallon, who played back to succumb lbw.

After tea Bailey held a catch worth going miles to see, even by transport in Melbourne. Hassett, who was batting belligerently, edged a ball from Brown low to the grass and Bailey grasped it one-handed, flinging the heart and soul of him at the chance. Brown's antagonistic bowling, which had disposed in rapid sequence Loxton, Lindwall and Hassett and changed the day's course, was all done with an old ball and less by the arts of length and variation of pace (which were excellent) than by vehemence of will and power of a good right arm. With every run invaluable and every ball a nail in somebody's coffin for certain – England or Australia's – a stand by Johnson and Johnston (only Iverson to come) came as more and more fuel to the flames of a game which burned and singed us as though all of us, crowd, cricketers, bats and balls and surrounding nature, were being caught up in the conflagration of an Australian midsummer. The ninth wicket added 25; Ian Johnson's portion was 23; and England tomorrow, so it was written, but mercifully we couldn't know it, would lose by 28. A day of irony, a day of cricket long to be remembered.

Brown again sent Simpson in first with Washbrook to begin England's task (if it couldn't be called a duty); a mere 179 to win a victory. It was a risky move surely, for if ever an

England innings needed a masterful lead it was now. But Washbrook was the first to fall, well beaten by Iverson with a ball that kept low. Hassett lost no time before he brought his spin-bowlers into action, but I fancy he was as hopeful of collaboration from the batsmen's fears or imaginings as from the wicket itself, which if it didn't reject spin, scarcely imparted the pace or 'snap' that kills. Bailey, sent in twenty minutes before close of play, was bowled by Ian Johnson for nothing, stretching forward to an off-break. Why was Bailey asked to bat in a position so responsible at the end of an afternoon on which he had not spared himself in the field? Hutton, who was possibly becoming accustomed to arriving at the crease not with a clean, confident sheet behind him but in the midst of falling wickets, dallied calmly with the last long agonising minutes, as the sun cast the shadows of the great stand over the grass in stark black blocks.

Denis Compton

From time to time, in most walks of life, a man appears who rises above his particular job and attracts the attention of people who are not intensely interested in his vocation. He has the appeal of what we conveniently call 'personality', though few of us are able to define the term. 'Handsome is as handsome does' is an old and very sensible saying, so true indeed that even a Denis Compton is obliged to prove his skill day after day, as he and the rest of us have found cause ruefully to realise only yesterday. It is, apparently, not enough that he should 'look well' and embody charm and appeal in all his actions in the field. Some cricketers, on the other hand, may show abnormal technique per-petually, breaking records by rote; yet they fail to achieve 'glamour' in an age that insists on it. Also, there's some-thing in a name.

Would our Denis seem to smell as sweet if it were Septimus Tomkinson? He has had all the help from the fairies in the cradle (though, of course, the fairies can take away capriciously, as well as give). He was baptised Denis Charles Scott Compton, a Barrie title, and he was born only a mile or two from Lord's in the month of May, the month when the cricket season blooms and blossoms; and his father not only loved the game but was good at it himself. He was endowed with sturdy loose limbs, square shoulders and strong wrists enlivened with suppleness. He was born with an inexhaustible flow of spirits and an eye that sees swiftly and can usually seek out the bright lining of a cloud; and not only that, it is an eye that wins friends at a glance. He is not tall but not short; just the right build, mingling the physical attributes of cricketer *and* footballer. Nature came to him with her cornucopia pretty full, and she let him help himself to it – for a while. Best of all, she brought to him a modest mind, without which the straight bat is only a symbol of vanity – not that Compton's bat is always straight. As we shall see, he has his own way of rendering first principles up to date.

Only the other year, it seems – time flies quickly in the cricketer's life, with wars ripping out whole chunks of summers – people going to Lord's and entering the ground at the W. G. Grace gates were buying scorecards from a bright-eyed boy, and he was Compton. Yes, his career has contained all the romantic ingredients: upward flight from the bottom rung. But no writer of a boy's story would risk a sudden eclipse of his hero at the height of his fame, in Australia too! Let us keep to the main pattern – 'Card of the match, sir'; then, at the age of eighteen, our hero is playing for Middlesex at Lord's, the historic place shaded by great ghosts; and all London around him on a June day, all granted him without a hard fight, gift added unto gift, the plant in the proper soil from the start. For in his first season he scores 1,004 runs, average 34.62. He gets a century in his sixth match. At the age of 20 he is chosen to play for England, and, facing Australian bowling in a Test match for the first time, he gets a century. War merely gives him the schoolboy's second wind; there seems no summit beyond his reach. He lowers the record of the one and only Jack Hobbs, 18 hundreds in one memorable summer. After beating at home the record aggregate in a season of Tom Hayward, 3,816 runs to the Old Master's 3,518, he goes on to score two centuries in a Test match against Australia, when he first plays there.

Today he is 33 years old and should have been rather in need of crutches. He throws off vicissitude without a shrug; he even throws off a sudden dreadful blow from his deceitful fairies, and throws it off without spite. He sometimes seems to trust his stars dangerously, grateful if they are ascendant but apparently scarcely aware if they are not.

But genius – even genius – needs to choose the right moment. Compton came to the high summer of his renown in a period when we all badly wanted the like of him on our fields for the purpose of rejuvenation. His cricket, in 1947, gave a nationwide pleasure which was somehow symbolical. In a world tired, disillusioned and bare, heavy with age and deprivation, this happy cricketer spread his favours everywhere, and thousands of us, young and old, ran his runs with him. Here at any rate was something unrationed. There were no coupons in an innings by Compton. He was contagious; he liberated impulses checked for long amongst all sorts and conditions of English folk – women as well as men, girls as well as boys. He embraced a new public in search of entertainment and release, a public which knows nothing of the old divisions that restricted sport to 'men's games'. Denis hath his fans not less dewy-eyed than those of Hollywood.

Is he a great batsman? I would prefer to describe him as a richly gifted one who is a stroke-player of distinction and some originality. He certainly isn't Hutton's equal in technique, and nature didn't intend that he should be. Hutton is obviously the more organised batsman of the two; he possessed what I call (and I hope I won't scare away my schoolboy) power of conception, ability to see a long way ahead in an innings. A big score by Hutton is thought out, or is the consequence of deliberation, either before or during the execution of it. Compton seems frequently to play according to mood, or what once on a time was called the inspiration of the moment. Hutton's cricket is old in the head, rational and responsible. Compton's cricket is never old in the head; for all its schooling and skill it simply will not grow up. If Hutton had run into half of Compton's appalling misfortunes in Australia during the Test matches of 1950-1951 he would have extricated himself by a severe bracing of the will. Compton was soon at a loss – an Aladdin who had forgotten how to rub the lamp and pronounce the necessary Abracadabra.

It is the failing of all sorts of criticism to consider an artist's or performer's technique apart from the individual who is using it, and to regard skill as a thing in itself which moves of its own volition and always in the same way. The truth is that if the technical equipment of Hutton could somehow be given to Compton, inoculated into his bones and being one night while he slept, and his own taken away from him, we should see little essential difference in his cricket next day. With Hutton we have the order and fulfilment of science; with Compton we have the short-cuts and spontaneous illuminations of temperament. Compton one day is so quick on his feet, in and out of the crease, that the bowler seems now and then to have to change his mind while running ball in hand to the wicket. Sometimes Compton prances down the pitch, only to find a length altogether too short for forward stroke; he will run back to cut it, and sometimes it is a scurry to save himself.

He is a superb driver between the left hand of mid-off and point. He is not always too particular about placing his left foot near the line of the ball: he is trustful of the enormous power and steering-wheel suppleness of his wrists. But on his ill-starred days he may very soon be caught because his bat has gone out to seek the ball on the off-side with no guidance apparently from Compton himself; it is

as an artificial limb. On these inexplicable days he falls
under that evil spell which reduces others not fit to tie his
laces to immobility of the right foot, so that, he, Compton,
yesterday as impertinent and ubiquitous of movement as
a young terrier tackling a mastiff, is bird-limed. Or his bat
has become leaden. Not often, though, is he so reduced and
chap-fallen. Yet, you see, the margin of error is there. He
needs always to be 'seeing' the ball with the clearest and
most rapid and comprehensive eye. A Hobbs or a Hutton,
because of sound grasp on the fundamentals, is able to go
on and on until the age of spectacles and ear trumpets.
Compton's cricket at his best belongs to youth.

He has, in fact, been called the Peter Pan of the game.
But the point about Peter Pan is not that he would not, but
could not grow up.

The operation on Compton's knee has been a serious
hindrance; still, I fancy that even if he hadn't incurred
this physical damage he would today just the same be under
the compulsion to face a transition period in his development as a batsman. As youth leaves us – and no man lives
for ever – we must overhaul our catechism, as that great
thinker, Captain Cuttle, advises. He has already proved
his harder metal. In Australia five years ago, on his first
visit there, he was put under the obligation of adopting a
method and outlook foreign to his nature as then supposedly known and revealed. He found himself bowed down
somewhat in heavy armour, his job grimly to 'hold the
fort'. Nobly, if not grimly, he obeyed the orders of the day,

and at Adelaide on a perfect wicket he was professionally clever enough to score 43 in two hours and a quarter, and compile two centuries in one Test match. At Trent Bridge in 1948 he defended a broken bridge for England for six and a half hours against Australians 'on the kill', while darkness fell on the earth from the sky. This innings was one of the greatest ever played in all the annals of Test cricket, both for extensive skill judiciously applied and for disciplined mind and temperament.

Maybe we shall not again look on the gay Lothario Compton of 1947; but let us console ourselves that 'ripeness is all'. He has the humour to adapt himself. When he first played Iverson at Melbourne in 1950 he was for a while completely at a loss; he tried all ways and means to deal with Iverson's peculiarly spun off-break, hopping about the pitch forward and backward, quite bereft, hitting and missing. At the other end of the wicket was young Sheppard playing Iverson in the middle of the bat. But as runs were not coming England's way and nothing being done to push the game forward, Sheppard between overs asked Denis for some advice or 'lead' in procedure.

'It's all right, David,' said Compton. 'Don't worry. You go on as you are, and I'll attend to the antics.'

When gloomy view was taken of his future, and on an afternoon that really did see him hobbling around Lord's on crutches, he told me he'd be playing again in a fortnight. 'You can't keep a good man down, can you?' he said without the slight affectation.

His wonderful year, as we all know, was 1947, in a season of glorious summer. When he came down the pavilion steps at Lord's on his way out to bat, the schoolboys crowed like cocks. An innings by Compton played this year of 1947 against Kent takes its place on the sunlit frieze of all that memory holds of gallant, accomplished and beautiful batsmanship. Kent declared on this enchanted afternoon and Wright bowled at his very best. Compton consumed him, leg-spinners, 'googlies' and all. His strokes were as shooting stars, gliding and skimming according to an astronomy of their own. The same sort of ball was treated in different ways and sent to different parts of Lord's. No effort, all grace; no flamboyance, but brilliance in the dress of courtesy. E. W. Swanton has written of this innings for the posterity of cricket.

He scored his last 71 . . . in 40 minutes. The Kent captain and his bowlers did not make the mistake of splitting the field. If they attacked the leg-stump they had six or seven men on the leg-side, or vice versa. But Denis countered every manoeuvre. Perhaps he would move sufficiently quickly to get outside the ball and chop it past slip, or, if the field were on the off-side, he drew the ball across his body to fine-leg. He was always on the move, either up the wicket or laterally and, as often as not, changed his direction as the ball left the bowler's hand.

When he got out, Kent quickly won the match, and so this great innings assumed the lustre which shines on bravely lost causes.

For my part I don't wish to think of Compton as one of the persistently masterful players. In spite of what recent trials and ordeals may have taught him, and in spite of the technical adjustments demanded by increase of years and some inevitable check on physical elasticity, he will never, I am sure, surrender to middle age. He will continue, at least this is the hope in the hearts of thousands of us, to convey the impression that he is capable, while batting, of

(1) making a superb stroke with his feet in the 'wrong' place;

(2) making a mighty pull while falling flat on his stomach;

(3) suddenly achieving a flawless execution so that the textbook black-and-white examples of Hutton seem to be given the illumination of colours;

(4) getting out to the easiest ball because after having gone halfway down the pitch he has forgotten exactly what he has ventured so far to do;

(5) running himself out or somebody else by yards, or

(6th and last) performing all these remarkable actions at one and the same time.

Denis Compton contributes to England life and holiday at the crown of the year; he is part of an English summer. In spite of his conquests, his record and scores, his cricket has always contained that hint of brevity which is the loveliest thing in the summer's lease.

Letter to the *Telegraph*, 1958

13 December 1958

Reflections on the Brisbane Display

SIR – Congratulations to my friend Mr E. W. Swanton on his brilliant and sensible comments from Brisbane.

'A bowler,' he reminds us, 'will only bowl as well as he is allowed to.' As one who once was himself a professional off (better than Burke!), may I heartily say, 'How right you are, Swanton!'

Various apologetic experts on the spot have assured us that it is unreasonable to expect our modern scientific batsmen to make strokes if:

a) the bowling is accurate;
b) the bowling is inaccurate;
c) there is too much grass on the wicket;

d) there is not too much grass on the wicket;

e) the field is set 'tight';

f) the field is spread out.

How do our contemporary heroes of the willow expect to receive the ball – on a plate with parsley?

Neville Cardus
London W1

Richie Benaud

At the beginning of June 1961, before the first Test match between England and Australia, Norman O'Neill, playing under Richie Benaud against Sussex, injured a knee while fielding, and was obliged to retire. At first the damage threatened to remove for some lengthy period this brilliant young cricketer from the Australian team. The news of O'Neill's and Australia's misfortune upset me so much that I wrote at once to Benaud hoping that O'Neill would quickly be fit again. I was as much concerned about the loss, even for a while, to the game of an artist as I was about this threat to Australia's chances of victory in the rubber.

The reply of Benaud to my letter was true to his character and to the character of most Australians. He thanked me for my sympathy but finished by saying: 'I'm not worrying unduly. I think that you'll find we'll be there when the chips are down.' And so, at the decisive moment in the rubber, they indeed were there. At Old Trafford, where the rubber's issue was settled, England were winning easily on the fifth afternoon, 150 for 1 wicket, Dexter riding the storm and only 106 needed now in as many minutes. Moreover, the Australian attack seemed pretty bankrupt: Davidson weary, Mackay physically handicapped. Benaud actually called for a breathing space, and drinks were brought into action, under a hot Manchester sun. (In 1934, two Australians were afflicted by sunstroke at Manchester during a Test Match.)

With the afternoon apparently lost for Australia, Benaud became a vessel of plenary inspiration. He bowled round the wicket and pitched his spin on the places on the pitch worn by Trueman's footmarks at the other end. As every cricketer and history knows, the trick came off. But it is not generally realised, even yet, how cleverly, how artfully, Benaud played it. He clean bowled the obstructive Subba Row the last ball, or thereabouts, before tea with a full-toss. He knew well enough that, an interval due, Subba Row would take no risk, offer no stroke, to a good ball. When Dexter was racing ahead, and defeat stared Australia in the face, Benaud said to himself, 'We can't possibly save this match but we *could* win it!'

He has been called a 'lucky' captain of cricket. The truth is that he, at his career's beginning, had to suffer hard blows to his confidence. At the age of 21 he played in his first Test match v West Indies at Sydney in January, 1952. He bowled only four overs, three balls and took Valentine's wicket for 14, of which number Valentine's share was exactly none. And he scored 3 and 19. His baptism to Test cricket in this country, in 1953, was scarcely memorable – three matches, five innings, 15 runs, average 3; 68 overs and two wickets for 174. He, supposedly a leg-spin bowler, failed to use the dusty wicket at Lord's when Willie Watson and Bailey retrieved a lost cause for England by hours of superbly dour defence. A famous player that afternoon was emphatic that Benaud never would reach top-class as a leg-spinner. 'He's a roller. Give him time,' I said. For I had seen young Benaud, months before this forlorn afternoon for him at Lord's – I had seen him in the nets at Sydney. Moreover, Arthur Mailey was putting faith in his potentiality as a back-of-the-hand spinner. But Benaud again disappointed his prophets during Hutton's and Tyson's triumphant invasion of Australia in 1954-55. He bowled 116 overs and 7 balls in the Tests for 202 runs and 10 wickets. And in nine completed innings he scored merely 148. For Australia in the West Indies, in 1955, he opened out his promise as a bowler, with 18 Test wickets, average 27.

Nonetheless, he was still on the doorstep of international achievement as recently as 1956, when he came to England for the second time. Another failure now could easily have seen the last of him amongst the Top People. He was nearing his 26th birthday. An Australian Test cricketer is usually established by this time of his life; in fact, many of them have looked towards retirement from the International scene by then – whatever Clarrie Grimmett may say to the contrary. Even in 1956, despite a resonant prelude to the season to the tune of an innings of 160 v Worcestershire, Richie for a while still could not raise himself above the level of the team's subsidiary resources. He was useful week by week, but in the first of the summer's Tests, at Nottingham, which had no result, he was not particularly useful. He scored 17, and bowled (in England's second innings only) 18 overs, and took none for 41. Between this and the second and Lord's Test he played in one match, scored 7 and 15 v Northamptonshire; and his one wicket cost 91. Conceivably he might not have been chosen for the Lord's Test if the Australian reserves had been stronger.

On the fourth morning of this match Australia, in a second innings, had lost six wickets for 115 and were only 229 ahead. On the evening before a morning on which Richie was destined to deal England a more or less death blow (with bat not ball), I met him for the first time at a dinner given by the most generous of hosts – John Arlott. We scarcely spoke. Benaud was not yet the confident Benaud of today. But there was a 'something' about him which impressed me, a suggestion of latent and alluring personality. The impression was strong enough to urge me to write an article, to appear before the game was resumed next morning, in which I risked a forecast ... 'Before we are much older Benaud will do something forcibly to demonstrate his natural and unmistakable gifts.'

Well, on this fourth morning, in a ticklish moment for Australia, with the day fresh and Trueman after blood with 4 wickets already rendering him even more than usually voracious — (4 for 38) — Benaud arrived at the ground almost late and had to rush into action at once, pads buckled breathlessly. Immediately he attacked, risking a long-armed drive. Also he hooked Trueman for six — and Trueman was the first of thousands to applaud the stroke. Benaud trusted to his eye daringly. In two hours twenty minutes he scored 97, swinging clean round the wheel of the game in the one engagement of the rubber won by Australia. This innings, maybe, marked the turn of his career.

I have gone into these statistics of Benaud's cricket to show how little indeed 'luck' has had to do with his development and progress. He, like any other man ever to do anything really well, had tested, not only in skill but in patience, philosophy and persistence. The only unmistakable good stroke from fortune to bless his onward course was at poor Ian Craig's expense, when this cricketer and captain of bright promise fell ill, and the Australian leadership passed from him to Benaud. With the swift resolution of something approaching genius, Richie grasped the chance. He directed Australia to victory in the rubber of 1958–59, in Australia. Seldom since then has he looked back. The entire world of cricket knows how he and Frank Worrell, by joint and imaginative agreement, saw to it that the Tests between Australia and the West Indies in 1960-61 produced some of the greatest and most thrilling and memorable cricket of our or any other time.

Richie, as befits an Australian and Sydney-sider, understands the value of realism. This good-looking captain of Australian cricket, with his frank eyes, and pleasant smile, scarcely fits at first sight into the general picture of an Australian skipper – think of dour immovable Armstrong, the lynx-eyed Herbert Collins, the shrewd, watchful Sir Donald. But Benaud is not wholly the cavalier batsman and the speculative leg-spinner (all leg-spinners must necessarily be speculative!). He knows that the time to be there is 'when the chips are down'.

His precious contribution to the game has been, of course, not his flair as a cricket captain; not even his ability to steer an XI to victory in a rubber in England, with a bowling team fairly to be called one of the weakest ever, Benaud himself an incapacitated member of it for weeks. No: Benaud has so far enriched cricket best by his leg-spin. This beautiful and difficult art, and any kind of spin if it comes to that, has been discouraged by legislation which has aided and abetted seam bowling. Any healthy, bodily fit, even brainless, young man can readily learn to swing his arm holding the ball's seam in his fingers the right way up. To master spin from the back of the hand, spin involving turn of the wrist and flick of fingers right to left – here is an art or craft calling for years of practice, and beautiful is it to watch a great leg-spinner, to follow the ball's seductive flight (or it might easily pitch halfway!) as it lures the batsmen forward, then drops on the earth; and it whips away or, the 'googly', comes back! Nothing mechanical here. Leg-spin insists on constant careful manipulation from its exponents – and constant concentration of mind.

So you see, this 'lucky' Benaud has not only fought through preliminary setbacks of form. While opposing them he also learned and mastered one of cricket's most skilful and enchanting arts, leg-spin with changeful flight that asks questions in the air.

Len Hutton

Len Hutton was the only batsman of his period to whom we could apply the term 'Old Master', referring in his case not to his number of years but to the style and vintage of his cricket. He followed in the succession of the classic professional batsmen who each went in first for his county and for England: Shrewsbury, Hayward, Hobbs and Sutcliffe – though Sutcliffe wore his classicism with a subtly Sutcliffian difference.

As Old Masters go, Hutton was young enough; the sadness is that physical disability put an end to his career in its prime. He had all the classic points of style when, not much more than 19, he came to Lord's in 1936 and scored 55. I then wrote of him in this strain of Cassandrian prophecy: 'Here is a young cricketer who is already old in the head and destined to enliven many a Lancashire and Yorkshire match of the future.'

If by means of some Time-machine capable of television

we could today see a picture of Hutton batting twenty years ago, and one taken of him during his maturity, we would notice no fundamental difference in technique. We would see that his cricket had grown in experience and finish, that is all. Like the music of Bach, Hutton's batsmanship in its evolution from an early to a late period presented no marked divisions; it was never raw, unprincipled or embryonic. He batted grammatically from the start, choosing his strokes as carefully as a professor of logic his words.

Even when he first played for Yorkshire, beginning with o, he seemed to begin an innings to a plan, building the shape and the duration of it to a blue-print in his mind, and to a time-table. But once in the greenest of his salad days he fell into error. He opened a Yorkshire innings on Saturday at Bradford with Arthur Mitchell, dourest and most unsmiling of the clan. After a characteristically Yorkshire investigation of the state of the wicket, the state of the opposition bowling, the state of mind the umpires were in, the state of the weather and barometer, and probably the state of the Bank of England itself, Mitchell and Hutton began to score now and then.

Young Hutton was feeling in form, so after he had played himself in he decided to cut a rising ball outside the off-stump. Remember that he was fresh to the Yorkshire scene and policies. He actually lay back and cut hard and swiftly, with cavalier flourish. He cut under the ball by an inch, and it sped bang into the wicket-keeper's gloves. And Mitchell, from the other end of the pitch, looked hard at Hutton and said, 'That's no——— use!' This was probably Hutton's true baptism, cleansing him of all vanity and lusts for insubstantial pageantry and temporal glory.

He observed the classical unities: that is to say, he did not venture beyond reliable and established limitations of batsmanship learned in the traditional school. Geometrical precision in the application of bat to ball, each movement of the feet considered until the right position was found almost instinctively, not bringing him merely to the ball and, as far as possible and if necessary over it, but also with body at the proper balance.

Never, or hardly ever, did Hutton play a thoughtless innings; his mind usually seemed to move a fraction of time in advance of his most rapid footwork and sudden tensions of limb, sinew and nerve. It is, of course, wrong to suppose that Hutton was at any time a batsman slow in his mental and physical reactions at the crease.

The scoreboard may have told us that he was not getting runs feverishly, but the vigilance of Hutton was eternal; the concentration in him was so intense that it frequently exhausted his not robust physique much sooner than did the more obvious toil and burden of the day. In the most austerely defensive Hutton innings we could feel a mental alertness; purpose in him suffered no weariness.

And whether or not he was putting into practice his wide repertoire of strokes, he was the stylist always; rarely was he discovered in an awkward position at the crease, rarely was he bustled or hurried. Once at Kennington Oval, Lindwall knocked Hutton's cap off in a Test match. Such an outrage could be equalled in a cricketer's imagination only by supposing that Alfred Mynn's tall hat was ever likewise rudely removed.

On a bowler's wicket, when the ball's spin was angular and waspish in turn, he could maintain his premeditated technical responses, often using a 'dead' bat, the handle held so loosely that when the ball came into contact with the blade's middle it was as though against a drugged cushion: the spin was anaesthetised into harmlessness.

But Hutton was, when grace descended upon him, a versatile and handsome stroke player. Old Trafford will remember that in 1948 he made a century of a brilliance which, in the circumstances – Bank Holiday and a Lancashire v Yorkshire match – was almost pagan.

He drove Lindwall with Spooneresque charm and panache at Brisbane in December 1950; at Lord's in the Test Match of 1953, he played one of the most regal and most highly pedigreed innings ever seen in an England and Australia Test Match on that hallowed ground. And he has contributed to a festival at Scarborough.

If Hutton had lived and played in the Lord Hawke epoch, when even Test cricketers in England had somehow to adapt themselves and their skill to matches limited to three days, he would have been a different batsman in his tempo and mental approach. But he could not possibly have been greater.

Any artist or master of craft is an organism in an environment; he is very much what circumstances and atmosphere make of him. His very greatness consists in how fully he can sum up the technique of his day as he finds it, and how representative he is of his day's spirit. MacLaren, lordly and opulent at the crease, was a representative man and cricketer in a lordly opulent period; Hutton's cricket has been as true as MacLaren's to the Zeitgeist, to the feeling, temper and even to the economy of the age which shaped his character and his skill, both conceived as much as in integrity as in joy.

As a captain he was shrewd but courteous; he knew the game's finest points and, though never likely to give anything away, was too proud to take anything not his due. Sometimes he may have allowed thoughtfulness to turn to worry; but this is a natural habit in the part of the world which Hutton comes from.

Hutton certainly showed that a professional cricketer can wear the robes of leadership in the field of play with dignity. At first, no doubt, he appeared at the head of his troops not wearing anything like a Caesarian toga, but rather the uniform of a sergeant-major. But he moved up in rank and prestige until he became worthy of his command and defeated Australia twice in successive rubbers, wresting one from the enemy at the pinch and looting the other after a series of Tests which were, if I may be free with my allusions and metaphors, the Australians' Austerlitz.

One of Hutton's most winning characteristics – and

his personality is extremely attractive – is his smile, a smile with a twinkle in it. He had many occasions in his distinguished career on which to indulge this smile, many provocations to it, and he never missed the joke. A Yorkshireman has his own idea of humour, and Hutton, as great or famous as any Yorkshireman contemporary with him, relished his laugh all the more because very often it came last.

Keith Miller

Keith Miller, an Australian through and through, is obviously an Australian at first sight, though not at the first sound of his voice, for he speaks English as it is pronounced, say, in Streatham. His appearance, the physical shape of him, is pervasive presence – he is pure eternal Australian, sun-saturated, absolutely 'dinkum'. See him in flannels, his wrinkled brow glistening with sweat, and surely you'll agree that he should inspire a sculptor to make an image of him to be erected in some public square in Canberra, there to stand down the ages as *Australia in excelsis*. I commend the idea to Prime Minister 'Bob' Menzies.

I could have sworn that he was a 'Sydney-sider', born near Randwick's racecourse. As a fact, he first saw the light of day in Melbourne, and so I suppose we must call him a Victorian. I came in good time to live in Sydney, where Bondi beach, Dee Why, Elizabeth Street and – of course — Randwick, acclimatised him, expelled all decorum and released any inhibitions acquired while dwelling in the elegant city of the Yarra. I have said always that Melbourne is Australia in a top hat and a starched wing-collar. Sydney is inclined to be raffish, uncollared, racy, even indifferent to manners that get in the way of natural impulse. The solidity of Melbourne, social and economic, has somehow been hinted at by most of her greatest cricketers — the sane, down-to-earth Armstrong, Woodfull, Ponsford, Hassett, McDonald, Ian Johnston, to name a few. Neil Harvey, a brilliant deviation from type, gravitated, like Miller, and as inevitably as needle to pole, to Sydney.

If we come to reflect on the matter, most of Australia's spectacular cricketers have been nurtured in New South Wales and tanned by the Sydney heat and the Sydney 'Southerly buster' — Trumper, Macartney, Bradman, Kippax, Andrews, Mailey, Jack Gregory, Archie Jackson, Johnny Taylor, Bertie Oldfield, McCabe, O'Reilly, O'Neill... Miller fits into the Sydney scene every inch of him. Merely to get a glimpse of him prompts me to see, with my mind's eye, Randwick, Castlereagh Street, 'Ushers' and the Domain and the long bar in the Australian hotel and the lovely sweep of the green oval of the Sydney cricket ground. ''Ow yer gow-in', Keith?' they hail him; ''E's dinkum, too right, 'e is.' In our time no Australian has vied with Miller for first place as a national hero and symbol.

Miller, nearly six foot tall, knows the almost forgotten secret these days of *panache.* Loose of limb with good shoulders, he is alluring in the eyes of the ladies who sit in the Sheridan stand at Sydney. In the Test match v England at Sydney in January 1951, Hutton and Simpson were well-rooted and the score 128 for 1. England had lost at Brisbane and Melbourne; the rubber was now at stake. Before this third Test, England had prayed to win the toss. 'Let us only bat first on a good wicket,' they had said. Well, England was, on this hot scorching afternoon at Sydney, batting first. And Hutton and Simpson seemed impregnable. The Australians were waiting without much hope for the new ball.

Ten minutes from tea, Miller had strayed from the slips to the outfield. He stood in front of the Sheridan stand. He was communing between one ball and the next with the ladies. Then Hassett, Australia's captain, called on him to send down a few overs, merely to mark time, till the interval and to give the other perspiring bowlers a rest. Miller reluctantly took the old ball, and at a deceptive medium pace relaxed like a fast bowler formally swinging his arm in the nets, he got rid of Hutton and Compton in an over, suddenly, from a short run, delivering streaked lightning. Immediately after tea he had Simpson caught at short leg. In 28 balls he took 3 for 5, and by sheer improvisation he won the rubber for Australia.

He was, in fact, a great artist in improvisation. When he bowled, he often ran to the crease from different places and always did he attack along a shortish distance. He couldn't bear to waste time. If a ball was played defensively from him he would clap his hands at the fielder retrieving the stroke, eager to 'get on with it'. At an inning's beginning his pace and bounce from the pitch were terrific and as though combustible. Certain England batsmen feared him even more palpitatingly than they feared Lindwall. He was 'at them' so abruptly, swinging round after his few impatient paces, his shoulders generating a last-second propulsive energy. 'If Keith had never gone in for batting', Cyril Washbrook one day told me, 'he would have been the most dangerous fast bowler ever.' He was quite dangerous enough. At Melbourne, he came close to equalling S. F. Barnes's wonder-bowling there, in December, 1911, when the Master took four wickets before lunch for one run, in five overs. Miller, at Melbourne in December, 1954, bowled throughout the 90 minutes before lunch, and took 3 wickets for 5 runs in 9 overs, despite a suspect knee. But when the mood to action visited Keith he was not conscious of physical impediments.

He was incalculable. Only mediocrity is always at its best. One day we would see Miller's bat trenchant and powerful, driving with a conquering swing, upright and free. Next day he might dismay us by pushing forward full stretch, groping at a good length ball, apprehensively groping. In 1945 he was the living embodiment of the game's and of London's resurrection from the ruin and the graveyard of the war. He came to Lord's, fresh from intrepid feats of battle in the air, and playing for the Dominions against England, enchanted the watching rationed English crowd by batsmanship glorious and visionary. He hit seven sixes and added 124 to a night before's score of 61 – in 90 minutes. An imperious drive off Eric Hollies landed on the roof of the broadcaster's box, but for which obstacle the ball would have cleared the pavilion, even as Albert Trott's gigantic hit had cleared it years previously.

Incalculable and unpredictable. One day he is in the slips interrupting conversation by a sudden leap or thrilling dive to take a sinful catch. Next day he is at cover, his mind wandering or pondering the 'odds' or the 'weights' and an easy chance, possibly from Washbrook in a Test, goes almost unnoticed by Keith, who hardly unfolds his arms. He is a law and lawless to himself. In fighting mood he could hurl a 'bumper' with the jubilant ferocity of a 'Digger' at Gallipoli throwing a hand grenade. In some other mood of his own fancy, he might go on to bowl like a middle-aged gentleman playing with young folk on the sands, rolling along donkey drops square-arm. During the course of F. R. Brown's England team's campaign in Australia in 1950-51 Miller promised on the eve of the third Test match at Sydney to play for me a dazzling innings tomorrow – 'if we win the toss. And if we lose it, when we bat I'll give you something to write about.' Then, against an England XI with an attack reduced by injuries to Bedser, Brown and Warr, he batted five hours for 99 in scourging sun.

In this same Australian summer of 1950-51 Victoria's spinner, Iverson, was a sore thorn in the sides of England's batsmen. On Sunday night as I was dining in Usher's Hotel, Keith dropped in and while we talked he asked, 'Why don't your chaps get into Jack Iverson and beat the hell out of him?'

I replied that it was easy for him to talk but it was 'our chaps', not Miller, who had to cope with Iverson.

'But New South Wales are playing Victoria next week,' responded Keith, 'come along and I'll show you.'

Show me he did: he flayed Iverson's attack, went down on the left knee and pulled off-breaks out of sight. Miller was not boasting as he spoke of Iverson's bowling and what should be done with it. In fact he was a great admirer of Iverson. But it is not in his mind or nature to understand submission to any obstacle or any antagonism. The stronger the odds in front of him the greater his relish of the game – game of cricket or game of life.

His technique as bowler or batsman could not be described as classic. The energy in him galvanised him to action which could not take the form of Lindwall's smooth poise and balance. Miller was the romantic, sometimes even the eccentric. With the new ball he could rap the batsman's gloves, even threaten the breastbone, from a good length. He could swing away very late at a pace which seemed to accelerate cruelly after the ball had pitched. I fancy his fastest ball was one of the fastest in all cricket's history. As a batsman he delighted the most critical eye whenever he was on the attack. Defensively, he prodded most gingerly. A certain great Australian batsman, now

dead, once startled me by saying of Keith as a batsman —
'He knows nothing about it really.' In other words, Miller
plays by intuition, making up all his strokes as he goes
along.

Certainly he never played as though cricket were a problem for mathematicians or a duty for the consideration
of moralists. If he lost his wicket to an absolutely crude
stroke, he would just shrug his shoulders, but without
contrition. In his Test match career, short and sweet, he
scored for Australia 2,958 runs, average 36.97, and took
170 wickets, average 22.97, proof of rare all-round powers,
seldom surpassed. Yet when we think of Miller now, we
don't dwell too much on his skill or on his performances.
It is the man, the Australian, the personality of him, that
we remember. This summing-up may seem trite enough,
but it's true. He was a virtuoso.

Possibly he didn't consciously *present* himself. He was
natural Keith when he tossed back his mane of hair, or
when, if a bowler stopped a return from him and made aim
as though to run him out, he would put forth an admonitory
hand at the aforesaid bowler. He was himself one morning
in a Test match at Sydney – he had just passed through the
gates on his way to the wicket to bat v England when a small
schoolboy ran after him, for his autograph. The gatekeeper,
scandalised, went immediately in pursuit of the schoolboy.
Miller waved the gatekeeper away, handed his bat to the
schoolboy to hold while he signed the autograph book.
Meanwhile sixty thousand people waited. Imagine the

small boy's ecstasy. Not only was he getting Keith's auto-graph: he was holding his bat while, in his eyes, all Sydney looked on. Keith was simply doing the natural thing: he could no more act unkindly to a schoolboy than he could be discourteous enough not to admire a pretty girl. At Lord's, on the Saturday evening of June 23rd, he had scored 30 and looked good for a century when he was caught at the wicket off a truly grand ball from Trueman. He at once raised his bat as a salute to Trueman. Another quite natural gesture of a cricketer who, with all his recurrent tantrums, was chivalrous opponent.

When I was a resident in Sydney, Keith for a while lived in the same block of flats as myself – in Crick Avenue, King's Cross, Montmartre – or shall we say the Soho – of Sydney. He would come up to my room and ask if I would play the gramophone for him.

'What record, Keith?'

Always he would ask for a piano concerto. Sometimes I would say, 'Why not a symphony this time?'

No: it had to be a piano concerto.

I imagine that he has scored hundreds of his runs and taken many, many wickets to the accompaniment, supplied mentally by himself, of the 'Emperor' concerto. The right music to go with his cricket at its greatest! Or perhaps something 'hotter' – say, Johnny and the Hurricanes.

Fact and Fiction in
the Search for Truth

Of the making of books about cricket there is no foreseeable end. Players compete with professional writers; players not accustomed to an intensive reading of books apparently find no difficulty about writing them. As far as I can gather, I am probably the only man in the profession who can't sit down at will and write a cricket book.

But an addition to the library, well worth while, has just come my way: *Sing all the Green Willow*, published by the Epworth Press at 25s. Don't let the title put you off, as easily it might. The book has truly been written by the author himself – Ronald Mason who, a year or two ago, produced a classic biography of the incomparable Walter Hammond. Ronald Mason, in this engaging book, writes on a variety of things, from Hornby and Barlow to P. G. Wodehouse and cricket. For purely personal reasons I was especially interested in the introductory chapter called 'The Truth about Cricket', because in it Mr Mason brings forward evidence that, long ago, while reporting a Lancashire v Oxford University match for this newspaper, I wandered or floated from actual fact to the higher Truth.

I described how Lancashire batted throughout a bitterly cold May day at the Parks. The day was so cold that Parkin, Dick Tyldesley, and the other tail-enders never left the warmth of a fire, never saw an Oxford bowler, until Dick went to the wicket half an hour before close of play, by which time Oxford's two really fast bowlers, Hewetson and Holmes, had spent their forces, so that Dick could lambast twenty or thirty runs off slow stuff. So much did Dick enjoy himself that, back to the warmth of the pavilion, not out, he said to me: 'Coom to ground early tomorrow, and Ah'll give thi summat to write about.'

Next morning, Hewetson, fresh and erratic, let fly at a terrific velocity, bang into Dick's bread basket, then whizzing past his head. Dick, next ball, retreated to the square-leg umpire and watched the total wreckage of his stumps. When I asked him what about the grand strokes he had promised, he honestly replied: 'Eh, Mr Cardus, Ah didn't know them two young buggers was playin'.'

Mr Mason has taken the trouble to investigate, and has discovered that Holmes and Hewetson played together only once against Lancashire in the Parks, and that on that occasion Dick Tyldesley went in late on the second morning and was caught off J. L. Guise. Moreover, Holmes did not bowl at all! Mr Mason is charitable; he notes the distinction between 'science' and 'Art'. The astronomer, he points out, can tell us all about a sunset but only a painter can tell us what it looks like. All very well; but in my mind's eye I can still, to this day, see Dick Tyldesley assaulted by Hewetson, see his vast rotundity shaken and toppled. And Mr Mason goes on to ask: 'Likewise with a number of other stories that, with the aid of this author's native genius' (meaning me) 'have passed into the language, about Barnes, or Brearley, or MacLaren ... Can we trust them, or him, at all?'

Before I plead guilty, m'lud, I'd like to point out that I have always tried to observe truth to character. And I was lucky, in my epoch, to have before me, every day, material for my work, a column every morning, wet or fine. One August holiday, completely wet and washed out at Old Trafford, I was welcomed by huge smiles by the Manchester *Guardian*'s chief sub-editor. 'Thank God,' he said, 'there's been no play – perhaps we can find some space for other events today.' But I had written an even longer piece than usual on what might have happened that day at Old Trafford had the weather kept fine for it.

Such cricketers as Parkin, Dick Tyldesley, Herbert Sutcliffe, Maurice Leyland, simply set the humorous or picturesque imagination free to go its way. Once, at Sheffield, Herbert Sutcliffe, glossy and immaculate, was fielding close to the bat. A terrific leg-hit struck him on the knee. Momentarily he winced, and bent down to rub the bruise. One or two of his Yorkshire colleagues solicitously

approached him; but Sutcliffe waved them comprehensively away; as though saying 'I am all right. We Sutcliffes
do not suffer pain.' True? How could I have invented
something so penetrating to the quiddity, the essence, of
the Sutclffe presence and temperament? These 'natural'
cricketers, pre-television and computer age, not yet stand-
ardised, simply prompted the reporter's sense of character.

It was, in respect of the inner and only truth, necessary
for the writer to go beyond the potential, to complete the
ripe human implications. For example: in a match at Old
Trafford, Dick Tyldesley apparently brought off a marvellous catch in the leg trap. (With all his assemblable bulk,
he had alacrity.) But, as the batsman was departing pavil-
ionwards, Dick called him back; the ball had just touched
the grass. I congratulated Dick, in print, on this act of
sportsmanship. Also, next morning I congratulated him
by word of mouth.

'Thanks, Mr Cardus,' he said: 'Westhoughton Sunday
School, tha knows.'

Did he really say it? To fulfil and complete him, to realise the truth of his Lancashire nature and being, it simply
had to be said. Whether he himself said it, or whether I put
the words into his mouth for him, matters nothing as far
as truth, as God knows it, is concerned.

I am myself often at a loss to remember if I am accurately
reporting an event or a saying. My hand on my heart, I
cannot be sure if Ted Wainwright, at Shrewsbury School,
once said to me, after I had asked him how did Ranjitsinhji

really bat — "E never made a Christian stroke in his life.' But I am able, on oath, to affirm that Wainwright's own words remain vivid in my memory, the identical words he used to describe an event at Lord's: 'Year before, Albert Trott hit ball reight over pavilion. Next year he set 'isself to 'it ball reight out of ground t'other end, into Nursrey. Ah were fieldin' near Nursrey sight-screen. Suddenly Albert lets fly, and oop ball goes, 'igh as Blackpool Tower . . . Ah loses sight of 'er 'genst black pavilion — then Ah see 'er agen, high as Blackpool Tower, mind you. An' Ah sez to myself, "Tha can catch it, Ted, tha can catch it.' Then Ah 'ad another look at 'er, and Ah said, "Oh bugger 'er," and lets 'er go. And Lord Hawke 'e cooms racin' over field, and sez, "Ted, why didn't you try to catch it?" and Ah sez, "Well, your Lordship, it were a bit 'igh, weren't it?"

I vouch also for the factual accuracy of the remark made to me in the press box at Brisbane at the beginning of a Test match between Australia and England. Sydney Barnes, the superb Australian batsman, and a true Sydney-sider, had retired from actual playing, and was now reporting. He sat behind me in the press box, and, before a ball was bowled, moved over my shoulder, saying, 'This is going to be an exciting rubber; and you and me, Neville, will have plenty to do — never mind these other blokes and their typewriters. Now, when you are hard-pressed, I'll take on from you. And when I am hard-pressed, you can take on from me. Similar styles, you know . . .'

A year ago Mr P. G. H. Fender expressed the opinion that

the public is discouraged from attending county matches by the press. Reporters, he argued, concentrated overmuch on statistics and technical fault-finding, and didn't write enough about the personality of the players, the scene and the atmosphere. By all means, a cricket writer should keep his eye on the ball, and give his readers the technical clues and explanations. But while he is describing how the ball 'moved off the seam', he should try to tell us what the bowler is thinking and saying, or what he is very likely to be thinking and saying, as he delivers the ball – especially if a catch is missed off it . . .

Walking Out of Lord's, 1969

ENGLAND V NEW ZEALAND, FIRST TEST, 1969

I could not have believed, a few summers ago, that the day was at hand on which I'd be leaving Lord's on a sunny day, after watching a Test match there for only an hour or so. I departed from Lord's last Saturday, bored to limpness, because I had seen Boycott and Edrich compile, or secrete, 100 runs from 56 overs, bowled by game, enthusiastic, inexperienced New Zealand cricketers. What would Boycott and Edrich have done confronted by Lindwall and Miller, Ramadhin and Valentine, Hall and Griffith?

In a full day, England, in a winning position versus a team not stronger all round than, say, Leicestershire, produced fewer than 300. Yet, on television, someone described the innings of Edrich as 'brilliant'. Had he, as he made this public pronouncement, forgotten Bill Edrich, who one day, on a spiteful 'green' pitch, flayed his spin within an inch of its life?

The poor, hard-worked TV commentators, those of them once upon a time Test match cricketers, did their best to gloss over the England batsmen's terribly tedius anonymity. Trevor Bailey referred to New Zealand's left-arm bowler, Howarth — he said he was 'operating' — as if he were a Verity come back to revisit the glimpses of the moon. (Mr Bailey usually refers to a bowler as 'operating' — probably, I am inclined to suggest, armed with an anaesthetic.)

All sorts of excuses for the England batsmen's sterility are put forward by the television commentators. Mr Laker informs us periodically that the ball is turning 'appreciably'. The commentaries go on like a chanted rubric. Motz is 'coming up' to bowl; Edrich 'plays him hard to mid-off, where so-and-so picks up — no run.' Hardly a hint of humour or irony on television: the radio chatterers are much brighter; they are free to take their eyes from the static, somnambulistic scene, and talk of irrelevant, and refreshingly irrelevant, things.

The prodding and 'tickling round the corner' persists every day on most first-class cricket fields in this country. And every day we hear the same justification for strokelessness: the ball is 'doing something off the seam', the wicket is 'green', or 'the ball is not coming off the bat'. I was brought up to believe that some physical propulsion, on the batsman's part, is needed to project a ball from the bat. The bowling, so we are told *ad nauseam*, is just short of a length; Bradman himself would, at his best, be 'kept quiet'. If you can believe all these 'scientific arrogances' you can believe anything.

Do the seam-short-of-a-length-devices check or 'keep quiet' the scoring strokes of overseas batsmen such as Goldstein, Richards, Ackerman, Pollock or Younis Ahmed? Does it paralyse Marner? None of these stroke players are half the equals of Bradman, Hammond, Compton, McCabe, each of whom would have watered at the mouth at the sight last Saturday of the attack (a technical term) of New Zealand's Taylor, Hadlee, Motz and Pollard. Howarth is undoubtedly a promising slowish left-arm bowler but, bless us, he was free to toss them up with no fieldsman behind his arm in the deep.

I remember a description of Charles Parker's spin on a dusty Cheltenham pitch, given to me by 'young' Joe Hardstaff, whose very presence at the wicket at Lord's on Saturday would have seemed to bring Derby breeding to a company of carthorses. He was then young, and he went in to bat for Nottinghamshire number six or so 'in the order'. He received the last ball of an over from Parker, which pitched on his leg stump then fizzed viciously across, just missing the off stump. So Hardstaff walked down the pitch to talk to George Gunn. 'I can't play this kind of bowling, Mr. Gunn,' he said, whereat George said: 'That's all right, son, just watch me for a little while.' And for half an hour Hardstaff had not to cope with another ball spun by Parker. Gunn kept him away from Parker.

Compensations of Viewing

The other morning, John Arlott came out with a most pregnant remark, more pregnant perhaps than intended: 'It has been suggested that the fact that only the last two days of the Lord's Test, and nothing at all of those at Trent Bridge or Edgbaston, was shown on television gave the impression that the cricket (in the England v Rest of the World series) was not worthwhile.'

I am reminded here of something said to me years ago by J. B. Priestley: 'If you are not on television, you don't count nowadays.' I have myself been on television – and have not received a single fan letter. Yet whenever I write, letters come to me abounding. Television appeals mainly to what George Meredith called 'the impressionable senses'; and *he* was known before the advent of television, and today reposes in the limbo.

Nonetheless, television has its uses for the lover of cricket unable, or disinclined, to go to watch an actual match. On the screen he misses the living panorama, but he can see what the ball is doing after it has left he bowler's hand and has pitched; he can see the turn or swing to an inch.

At Headingley last week the television commentators unanimously agreed that Sobers was bowling 'magnificently', with 'no luck': 20 overs, 11 maidens, 24 runs, no wickets – nary a wicket in nearly two hours' individual work. As a once-in-a-time bowler myself, I do not believe that anybody can bowl 'magnificently' for 20 overs without taking a wicket. I happened to scrutinise the bowling of Sobers on television during his delivery of these 20 overs. Time after time he swung the ball outside the batsman's danger-zone; he could often be 'left alone'.

I recall a stern observation of the incomparable Sydney Barnes as he looked at a bowler 'moving' the ball a foot or so away from middle stump past the off stump, from middle past the leg stump. 'Why', queried the Master, 'does he not keep the batsman playing? I never give 'em a moment's piece.' Barlow got his wickets at Leeds by a threatening line of flight, with not too much swing. The new-ball obsession has reduced the efficiency of more than one top-class bowler I could name.

I wish we could go back to the old-time rule which allowed the use of one and the same ball throughout a team's longest innings. As Jack Gunn said, with rueful ripe flavour, 'Aye, we 'ad to mek do with same ball unless it come in two.' With an old ball shineless, almost seamless, Tom Richardson took 1,000 wickets in four consecutive seasons, bowling fast on the flawless Oval wickets of 1894–1897.

The television and radio commentators wax warmly and sympathetically about some bowler's endurance: 'This is his twenty-fifth over, and he must be tiring.' At Old Trafford in July 1896, Richardson bowled without rest for three hours for England v Australia. In his thirty-fourth year E. A. Macdonald took 205 wickets for Lancashire, in 1,249 overs. For all the talk about over-worked first-class cricketers, no bowler gets through 1,000 overs in a summer. But no bowler of 1970 has the perfect action of a Macdonald or Richardson, though Snow is an example of finely accumulating rhythmic movement. And there are possibilities of a Trueman sort of dynamic onrush in the action of Ward of Derbyshire.

The fact about these England and the Rest of the World matches is the players in them include some of the most gifted, the most fascinating to watch, ever to be seen in all my long experience of cricket. Jessop himself was not more exciting, more creative, at the crease or in the field than Clive Lloyd. I have seen him make strokes which have caused me to catch breath – a pull square for six from a ball rising awkwardly on his off side. He is violent, Wagnerian, with the wonderful relaxations of Wagner.

Sobers, as batsman, is entirely and easefully musical. He performs his wonders without rhetoric, without strain. He puts the bloom on the orthodox. There is an impersonal air about his batsmanship, a certain self-detachment, as though he were spreading his genius over the field like a disinterested spectator.

Frank Woolley had the same kind of aloofness. It is as though Sobers, as Woolley did, takes his gifts for granted and thinks no more of them, phenomenally, than of the continuous motions and functionings of his respiratory organs. The art that conceals art. But I am often at a loss why, when a tail-end batsman confronts Sobers as a bowler, he sends down to him balls which the said tail-ender is not clever enough to play.

Then there is the magic of Kanhai, the configurations of Intikhab, alluring to the spectator whether he is getting wickets or not. There is the gusto of Barlow, hugging himself whenever he breaks a partnership. And there are Mushtaq, Richards, Procter, all endowed with personal identity, ready to give rein to inborn talents. Never was cricket more generously dowered by inimitable skill and personal presence than in this Rest of the World XI.

And what of the England team for the personal play which goes beyond, and cannot be reflected in the scoreboard? Boycott has class, so has Cowdrey – in form or not. Knott, behind the stumps, is unmistakably himself, alert, ever exercising, ravenous of appetite. The other England cricketers of the moment are admirable craftsmen, good batsmen, bowlers and fieldsmen. Do they hold me, so that I cannot take my eyes from them, on television or on the field of play, for a moment? Frankly, no. The reason for this finely competent anonymity? I don't know.

Cricket's Transmogrification

Cricket has been obliged to change over the decades in technique and manner, obliged to alter as it alteration found – if I may be Shakespearian and platitudinous at the same time. But in the main, the game, in its broad outlines, has remained recognisable at first sight: batsmen have gone through traditional motions, bowlers and fieldsmen too; and umpires have administered law in much the same way, though the old long stately coast has gone, more or less, causing the Dogberrys of cricket to assume the clinical aspect of dental surgeons, in wear of shorter, severer cut.

If Frank Woolley had been present at Kennington Oval the other week, watching Sobers, he could well have felt time had turned in its tracks and he himself was in full play again, at the turn of the century. And if, also at Kennington Oval last week, Cyril Washbrook had been present, as spectator, he could justly have exclaimed, witnessing a square cut by Intikhab, 'There by the Grace of God go I!' It was probably the first great square cut executed by any cricketer since Washbrook and the Australian Sydney Barnes.

It is not in the field of play, so much as in the Press Box, that cricket's aspect and procedure have been, as the man in Dickens says, transmogrified. The Press Box today is a populous, efficiently statistical concourse of accountancy and sleepless vigilance, typewriters in perpetual motion, some of them tapping away as though on the padded surfaces of half-cooked steak puddings.

When I myself first ventured into a Press Box, told to occupy the back seat to begin with, not more than five or six scribes were in it to report an everyday county match. No television and, for radio, only the resonant Gobbi-toned voice of Howard Marshall to speak from time to time. Silence reigned supreme. There was no specialist statistician to inform us that so-and-so had bowled so many overs, or that so-and-so had completed his 50 in two and a half hours. We had to make our *own* statistical recordings. Jimmy Catton, of the now defunct *Manchester Evening Chronicle*, himself wrote down a ball-by-ball analysis of each bowler, also detailing the value and direction of every stroke. So did all the other cricket reporters.

Also, they wrote in a traditional prose, employing sentences to fit certain occasions, with the reverence and repetitiveness of *rubric*. For example, the last batsman of a team always 'whipped in'. I particularly loved the phrase,

'Tyldesley, having driven Hirst for four, turned his attention to Rhodes.' 'Turned his attention to' – why, the echo of this language brings back, ages after, the vision of J. T. Tyldesley on the attack.

Other conventional phrases handed down in the old Press Boxes, father to son, included, 'Hobbs was guilty of obstruction.' Dear Jimmy Catton, small, rubicund and rotund, was the first of the old school to experiment with venerable clichés. He once wrote, 'Maclaren drove Noble for the full complement,' which, of course, appeared in print, 'for the full compliment'. Ronnie Simmons, a reporter daringly *avant garde*, one day at Lord's risked airing his knowledge of German in his report. 'Jim Smith', he wrote, 'drove a ball from Fender into the *Ewigkeit*'; meaning that the ball had been dispatched into the blue of eternity. He was naturally frustrated to read, next day, that Jim Smith had driven a ball from Fender 'into his wicket'.

I also began studiously to take these notes of accountancy on my first appearances in the Press Box. At Lord's, I dared not for a summer to venture into the Press Box *at all*. I felt I had not yet graduated, was not ready to go into the presence of Sydney Pardon, All-Father of *Wisden*, who watched cricket through tiny ivory-covered opera glasses, which he used night after night at Covent Garden Opera to look at Frida Leider and Tetrazzini. I used to write my reports sitting on the Green Bank at Lord's at the base of the Old Press Box next to the Pavilion. Pardon saw me at

work there one afternoon, and insisted in taking me up to
the Press Box and introducing me to the members – I mean
the Life members – Hubert Preston, Stewart Caine, Harry
Carson. They bowed to me: it was like a levee.

I adored Pullen ('Old Ebor') of the *Yorkshire Post*, once
described by Lord Hawke as Yorkshire's Twelfth Man.
Pullen never saw Peel and Wainwright, and never really
accepted 'modern' methods. Whenever George Macauley,
superb off-spinner, went on to bowl over the wicket, then,
seeing the ball nip back inches, went round the wicket,
Pullen would invariably report that Macauley, 'obviously
having difficulty in maintaining a foothold, was obliged to
bowl round the wicket'. I would spoil this gorgeous story if
I were to give away the technical clue.

All the reporters of my early salad days travelled up
and down the land with our respective cricket teams – by
train, not individually and alone by car. So we became
a community, the players knew us, and we knew them.
None the less, our cricketers retained independence,
which we, the reporters, shared. One Saturday evening,
in a Lancashire and Yorkshire match, at Old Trafford,
Richard Tyldesley suddenly lost his length and 'sent
down' some dreadful and expensive overs, at a critical
point of the proceedings. I dealt with this lapse rather
severely in my *Manchester Guardian* notice (1,500 words
at least). I saw Harry Makepeace on the Monday morning,
and he said to me, 'We've just shown your article to Dick.
He read it, then threw the paper down on the table and

said, "Ah'd like to bowl at bugger."' The right and proper professional retort.

There was also, in the old Press Box at Old Trafford, Johnny Clegg, of the *Manchester Evening News*. One of his phrases comes back to my mind with eternal freshness: 'The game was held up by a shower of rain; and on resumption, Parkin had recourse to the sawdust.'

During this period of cricket's history, the players were known as Amateurs or Professionals, even as Gentlemen and Players. The poet Craig, at Kennington Oval, would go about the crowd selling his broadsheets, assuring us, in deliciously Cockney sententiousness, 'all the Gentlemen are players, and all the players are Gentlemen.' In the reports of *The Times*, of the period, an amateur player was always named with the affix 'Mr'. Thus: 'Mr Warner drove Hirst for four.' All an Australian XI were addressed, in a *Times* report, as 'Mr —'. 'Mr Jones bowled at a great pace.' Jones was a typical Aussie, dinkum as Melbourne ale.

Into the Press Boxes of the ancient years – circa 1920–1930 – tea was actually served at 4.15, by a white-ribboned waitress, at sixpence a head. As I say, on quiet sunny afternoons silence would reign supreme in the Press Boxes, as we wrote out our reports, on telegraph forms (80 words to the page, each in a framed space). It was my practice to dispatch 800 words at the tea interval, and another 500 or so at close of play.

There was a lot to write about then, from Old Trafford to Dover, but not much more, either in number of words or in adjectival power of words, than could today be written about the cricket of Marshall, Intikhab, Clive Lloyd, Lancashire's Pilling, and Lancashire's (and/or Yorkshire's) Wood, and Kent's Denness, and Surrey's Edwards, and Snow of Sussex. The game was always as good as it used to be.